"Millions of men are living lives of quiet desperation. By some measures, it's never been easier to be a man, yet the rates of male depression, addiction, and suicide suggest otherwise. The modern era is replete with paradoxes. Men are simultaneously told to man up and to man down. To be emotionally vulnerable yet stoic. To protect, provide, and sacrifice but not to expect authority, respect, or even kindness in return. Mark has experienced both great victories and painful defeats firsthand. In this insightful book, he provides a straight-talking yet compassionate framework for men who are battling inner and outer demons."

—Zuby, Author, Rapper, Podcast Host

"Spirituality is for everyone, and it looks different for everyone, including men who have achieved business success at incredible personal costs. Often, attachment issues from childhood together with addictions developed later in life can hide or mask the true man. He knows this. He is looking for an authentic path to inner truth without self-deceit. Mark Gogolewski's book is the way."

—Danielle Delaney, ThD, President/Founder/CEO, Danielle Delaney Counseling Inc. and Crisis Intervention Counselor

"The current culture blames men not only for their own troubles but also for everyone else's. So it's no surprise that we see men struggling with addiction, loneliness, and despair. But as men, we have the ability to dig deep, face our demons, and come out transformed. And it's easier with help. In this book, Mark tells his story and gives the advice and guidance that men need. Because Mark's *been there. He knows.*"

—Jason Andrews, Hypnotist and Coach

"Spirituality for men, by men, is completely missing from our culture. Instead, we have shame. Mark Gogolewski takes a great stride on the journey to fix that, with his new book. It's for every man searching for answers but doesn't know the question."

—Zeeshan Hoodbhoy, MD, Founder/CEO of NCLEX High Yield

"I've interviewed many of the most influential men in America and around the world, and what stands out is the story behind their success. Beneath the surface, many have traded inner peace for outer achievements—and it shows. My friend Mark Gogolewski knows this journey firsthand. He's lived it, lost it, and discovered a path to profound spiritual fulfillment. Every man needs to read this book."

—Dave Rubin, Host, *The Rubin Report*

HOW TO BE
OK

HOW TO BE OK

(WHEN YOU'RE SUPPOSED TO BE OK BUT YOU'RE NOT)

MARK GOGOLEWSKI
OK AND MORE
Tahoe City, CA

This book is for informational purposes only. It is not intended to serve as a substitute for professional advice. The author and publisher specifically disclaim any and all liability arising directly or indirectly from the use of any information contained in this book. A professional should be consulted regarding your specific situation. Any product mentioned in this book does not imply endorsement of that product by the author or publisher.

All rights reserved. No part of this book may be used or reproduced in any manner whatsoever without written permission of the publisher, except in the case of brief quotations embodied in critical articles or reviews.

How to Be OK copyright © 2025 by Mark Gogolewski
OK AND MORE

P.O. 5548
Tahoe City, CA 96145
www.markgogolewski.com
Send feedback to info@markgogolewski.com

Publisher's Cataloging-in-Publication
    Names: Gogolewski, Mark, author.
    Title: How to be OK : (when you're supposed to be OK but you're not) / Mark Gogolewski.
    Other titles: How to be okay : (when you are supposed to be okay but you are not)
    Description: Tahoe City, CA : OK and More, [2024] | Includes bibliographical references.
    Identifiers: ISBN: 979-8-9918731-2-3 (hardcover) | 979-8-9918731-1-6 (softcover) | 979-8-9918731-0-9 (ebook) | 979-8-9918731-3-0 (audiobook)
    Subjects: LCSH: Men--Psychology. | Self-realization. | Self-acceptance. | Spiritual healing. | Type A behavior. | Addicts.
    Classification: LCC: HQ1090 .G64 2024 | DDC: 155.332--dc23

> **Special discounts for bulk sales are available.**
> Please contact info@markgogolewski.com.

My dear sons, when I was lost in the dark, you two were my light.

you are the promise

you are the gift

you are the secret

you are the prayer

you are the

you are

you

by Mark Gogolewski

CONTENTS

Foreword XIX
Chapter 1: Cut to the Chase. 3
Chapter 2: Normal Again. 15
Chapter 3: The Origin Story of Who You're Not . . . 31
Chapter 4: Forgiving the Man You Weren't. 51
Chapter 5: Release from the Past, into the Present . 67
Chapter 6: Every Man Is an Island. 83
Chapter 7: Mascluine Spirituality. 103
Chapter 8: Reaching OK 125
Epilogue: Better Than OK. 137
Acknowledgments. 147
About the Author 153

TELL ME WHAT YOU THINK

Let other readers know what you thought of *How to Be OK*. Please write an honest review for this book on your favorite online bookshop.

★★★★★

FOREWORD

Men who are willing to dive deep into their own spirituality, their own power and lack of power, their own vulnerability and lack of vulnerability are few and far between. When a man does venture in, we can only hope that he has the wherewithal to return and communicate what he has found to other men . . . and to women as well—in that way giving guidance to some and apologies and explanations to others.

Mark Gogolewski's book is a guidebook written by a guide. I say this because many so-called guidebooks are only someone's idea of what the journey to true compassion looks like. A book written by a true guide means that the author has walked the territory and not the map, which makes a world of difference. For one thing, and perhaps one of the most important things, it means that the guide has found a way to unite failure and success into a real, ongoing life rather than a continuation of the eternal ups and downs that quick fixes tend to bring. This is what sets this book apart: It is a book of healing. So what the reader reads is a healing journey, a voyage of the body, mind, and spirit, rather than an idea, a concept, or just a thought of what could be. This makes *How to Be OK (When You're Supposed to Be OK But You're Not)* an earthbound book. It doesn't promise the moon, but it delivers an evening sky. It doesn't promise all-encompassing illumination, but instead brings daylight where before there was only endless dusk and a half-lit life. It is, above all, a human book and not a book written by some idealized superman. This is its secret sauce.

Near the end of his volume, Mark says that this book is really one big prayer. This is an important and potent statement. Although most people think of prayer as a way of talking to the invisible, whether you call that invisible God or spirit or something else, prayer is really an invitation to be in a relationship with the mystery of life. Who do we pray to when we pray? Really, we don't know. But Mark suggests, simply by the existence of this book and the journey he has been on, that he is praying to Life Itself and that he trusts life itself to bring to fruition the human instinct for wholeness, the ongoing, never-finished, sometimes difficult, always rewarding search for, and finding of, wholeness.

Mark has been a student of mine for many years. In addition to being a successful businessman, Mark has always been a spiritual seeker of truth. In this book he shares his journey to more self-awareness as he continues to discover who he is in all the facets of his life and what this life is about. I've watched Mark as he continues to change and grow, fulfilling the destiny his own heart has given him. I hold him dearly in my heart, as I know you will as you read his journey.

Let me be the first to invite you to take this journey with Mark through spiritual darkness into spiritual day. There's a lot to see.

—Myōgen Jason Shulman
Founder, A Society of Souls

CHAPTER 1

CUT TO THE CHASE

You think you're here to feel better. But you're really here to learn the truth.
—Colette, Healer

What the fuck? I had no idea what Colette was talking about with this truth thing.

Colette was an energy healer or Reiki master. Or was it Reiki mistress? No, too weird. It was all too woo-woo for me anyway. And yet curiosity brought me back after the initial session. And kept me coming back. I was there in the first place for the usual reasons: *Why am I so miserable?*

Why am I acting this way? Is this my fault? All my fault? Divorce? Drinking? Drugs? What I'd been doing to deal with it wasn't working at all. Everything was backfiring. I thought I deserved to be happy. You know . . . fun. Pleasure. The good life. It was all masks.

They call it a midlife crisis for a reason. I felt like a ridiculously expensive sports car careening toward the side of a mountain.

Colette was my latest stop on an erratic search for something. For *the* thing. Anything, really. I had to get over the misery. Get past the suffering. Life was not what I wanted it to be or thought it could be. Force of will had been unable to bring about change. Force of will always runs out. Always. Then you get unforced errors. Addiction, accelerated by the local drinking culture. Then chasing high-risk pleasure like skydiving to gambling to Burning Man. There were lower-risk activities as well, like desperately searching for a retreat away from my madness, trying my turn as a ski bum, and volunteering time to my community. Then I got bored, down to my bones.

Selling a software company gave me options to start new businesses, half failing one after the

CHAPTER 1 - CUT TO THE CHASE

other. The other half failing to fill the hole in my heart. I attended personal development seminars and groups with good ideas but slapdash methods, delaying the inevitable falling apart. My marriage had also been falling apart, and things were over. My life became captured by divorce. I drank more during those two years. I went too far and physically couldn't stop. Then there was no stopping. So I went to detox—a three- to seven-day cold turkey rehabilitation. It had to be quick. I needed to be there for our kids, present, especially because the divorce was not yet final. I didn't want to stop drinking; I wanted to stop drinking *too much*, whatever that meant. I wanted to stop screwing up and not lose the life I had built. I realized in detox that these days of cleaning up might not work out when I met people there for their fourth, fifth, ninth time. I swore to myself I would be different, and a quiet, deep voice laughed at my arrogance.

The journey continued. I was sober more days than I drank. I slipped again and again. I went to detox again and again. It was maddening. I thought maybe if I found the right religion or spiritual path, the right healer or guru or meditation coach, or the right book or chapter to quote about God—devotion or ascetic practice—I would find the answer. The answer was out there, and I *had to find it*. I did not find it. I only found myself depressed. Then one of my best friends with matching struggles shot himself. He had the beautiful house, the wonderful wife, the loving kids, and he ended it all. I would do anything not to feel this way again. I was broken. I knew no way out.

• • • •

You're probably continuing with this book because you felt something reading the opening to this chapter. Maybe you felt a lot of things. You might have seen parts of yourself in this story. You're in a community with more people than you think. You are now where I have been. And self-help solutions and spiritual quick fixes, although well-meaning approaches, haven't been enough. Well, I've got bad news for you: There is no solution. There is not *one* solution, anyway.

You think you're reading this book to feel better. But you're really reading it to learn the

CHAPTER 1 - CUT TO THE CHASE

truth. It took me ten years to understand that. I wrote this book to shorten your learning curve so that you can skip years of misery and suffering. You'll have to live it. Your only way out is through, regardless of your starting point. Regardless of the specifics of your pain. But when you realize all that you are not—when you eliminate what you believed you should be, do, or become—life gets a lot clearer. Superficial pursuits fade away, and you find yourself drawn naturally to what gives you lasting meaning.

You start to like yourself. You actually like yourself. Really. You come to understand what I thought for years was complete bullshit: self-love. That felt like a nice thing to say when there was nothing else. I just wanted to feel better. Yet the truth was in the trite. That's what I didn't understand, for many years. But you can, and sooner than that. It is possible to find peace of mind within yourself, not outside, and it may come easier than anything you've tried so far. You want to be happy, but you've been hurting and need the hurt to stop. It can stop. I wrote this book to help you find what my friend never did but desperately needed and what I feared was not possible.

I will help you feel OK again. That's it.

I will help you feel just OK.

I am not promising enlightenment or cloud nine joy states all day or drug high–like feelings of nonego existence and whatever else is promised on a man's search for healing. This is not a quick path, but if you've tried everything else and none of it has worked, maybe it's time to try something—rather, to aim for something—else.

You should aim for OK. Here's why I can say this.

I've been through several seasons of my life and different struggles. The various sufferings that I have endured are relatable to a significant percentage of the population. What people are looking for is a breadcrumb trail in the direction of lasting solutions and relief from the suffering. The specifics may differ, but the struggles are shockingly universal.

The state of okayness is the most valuable because it's the most difficult to achieve for people who are so far away from it, right?

CHAPTER 1 - CUT TO THE CHASE

There are the states of transcendence and oneness and joy and blah, blah, blah. But people who are having a hard time with the pain and challenges that I have endured, be it issues with a father wound, relationships with growing and grown children, with a spouse turned former spouse, to addictions, to mental health issues, to all of these things that I'm sharing and the various solutions that I have found, what people are looking for is both what to do and what not to do. Yet not in a how-to way but in more of a what's-been-tested way.

I also realized there's this weird thing of wanting one thing to solve, to fix everything, and there is value in sticking with something, but there's absolutely no way that one thing can solve it all. A lot of gurus don't realize that. This book is a journey memoir that shares the lessons I learned that I wasn't ready for when I first learned them and then how I finally became ready for them.

How do you know that the state of okayness, as we'll call it, is possible—for someone like you—by reading some dude's book? Seriously, come on. It sounds too good to be true, I sure would think. Let me show you what to expect. This may ease your mind.

You know about dieting, of course. A diet, like a motivational seminar, is a seasonal thing. It's what you do when you know something has to change, but you're not sure what, exactly, is going to work best, so you just do something. The idea is a radical commitment to a one-off experience. A phase, to get things going in the right direction. It's outward change without inward accountability, to use unnecessary spiritual language—but hey, there's a lot of that ahead, so deal with it. Diets and seminars work the same— they work as long as you're on them and in them, respectively. They demand force of will to succeed. As soon as you stop, pause, cheat, or go home, it's so over. You yo-yo, crash, put it all back on, feel sad and angry and disempowered again. "Just tell me what to do" was why we did it, and we got what felt like an answer, but as soon as we were off the strict meal plan or out of the conference room and back home surrounded by the status quo once again, whatever direction we bought is gone. We are left drowning in feeling worse. And we know there is something wrong.

CHAPTER 1 - CUT TO THE CHASE

I was damn sure that something was me.

For many, and perhaps for you, this feeling is painfully familiar.

Here's the way out. It's a tougher decision. It's to be your own diet coach and your own motivational guru. It's the inner stuff. It's the hard work we hear trainers and experts and authors and healers and pastors and priests or priestesses and shamans talk about. Then they invite you to commit to their way. I'm not asking you to do that. In fact, I am specifically asking you not to do that.

I am asking you not to diet; I am asking you to choose the way to eat so that you'll be able to eat for the rest of your life without thinking about a meal plan ever again. Make it a habit. Make it who you are. You never have to read a health book or listen to a nutrition podcast or pay any attention to the latest scientific studies—none of that. You are enough. You are . . . OK. And you stay OK.

This is the best and worst news at once. What could be more true than facing the cold, hard fact that you have nowhere to go? Seek help all you want, but you can only count on being you. This is disheartening at first but completely liberating when embraced. Over the course of the upcoming chapters, we will do a little embracing together.

This is not a life optimization book. This is a life acceptance book. It will help you realize who you are, who you really are, what you are, what that means, and how to finally be OK with that. This is my promise to you. I'll help you by sharing my misadventures and missteps along my own way to get there, to the here that is the state of okayness. You will feel like yourself again for the first time ever. The past will slip back into the past and stay there. The past will no longer be chasing you. You will no longer be chasing after it—missed opportunities or the good old days lost but desperate to be relived. You will feel better, but first you will feel worse. Because you'll learn the truth.

The only way out is through, and I assure you it's possible. In fact, it is what you have been yearning for.

Just as you are expecting something of me as the author of this book, I, too, am asking something of you. I am asking you to decide to walk this walk to okayness with me. I am asking you

CHAPTER 1 - CUT TO THE CHASE

not to just want to feel that way. I am asking you *not* to want to just feel better or feel anything else. I am asking you *not to want* to stop acting poorly—drinking, eating crap, wasting time on useless hobbies, deprioritizing kids. Fuck *want*. I am asking you to *decide* that you will be OK again, or for the first time.

If your decision is yes, turn the page. I'm with you. Let's stop seeking and start finding.

CHAPTER 2

NORMAL AGAIN

Life is about choices. Some we regret, some we're proud of. Some will haunt us forever. The message: we are what we chose to be.
—Graham Brown

I wanted to feel normal again.
Welcome back, my friend. Yes, I feel normal again. Sigh. A flood of relief. A bit of fun too.

I just need to keep a cap on it. Praying I can leave in the past the struggle to stop because I damn well didn't want to. Well, I wanted to, but I didn't. Actually, maybe this wasn't *all* a problem. I *need* this. Just for a bit. It helps: *Here, ah. There. Keep it contained. Everything will be fine. Agreed. Right? For once? Please?*

I was angry, bargaining, and denying. I was swimming in my chaos. All the stages of grief were out of order, all at once.

The universal struggle is this emotional roller coaster, not the particulars of your addiction. For you, that opening story from the last chapter could be about drugs, sex, food, or booze. In today's age, it could be about porn, video games, or doomscrolling. It's about our redline experience and egocentric living at 110 percent. YOLO, mofo. Nobody can keep this up forever while close relationships are crashing and burning.

In the experiences of substance abuse, I found relief. I also found true fragments of my real self; just enough to keep doing it. You are doing the same with yours too. Let's be honest, among us at least.

This endless cycle is one massive protection plan, relief from your pain and wounds. It's about escaping from the past and into something else. For me, it was an escape from what I held on to most, what I suppressed, anchored in my

CHAPTER 2 - NORMAL AGAIN

fury and pain going back to childhood. With defenses up in one area, defenses are projected and discovered everywhere. I wanted to fight something.

Our responses don't make rational sense. It's a distraction, what we do, but also a gateway. We feel not OK afterward, or worse. But it feels worth it in that moment, maybe even a necessity. It might make you feel looser than your normal type A existence, deeply anxious all the time, stressed out. So you feel relaxed. You feel comfortable. You feel more positive than not, in the moment and after. But it's not just generic stress but actual suffering, and then you need it, whatever *it* is for you, to withstand the enduring pain, the acute situation.

The short-term benefit eclipses everything else, especially the long-term pain and payment.

Doing your thing, the relief probably makes you feel free. It might even make you feel creative. You might feel like yourself again. But you know as well as I do that our thing leads to not-so-great decisions. It leads to a lack of discipline and structure. And so you're not OK afterward with what you gave up, and long term it's more than not OK. Then it goes too far, and you are more a possession of the thing than you possess it. So you are definitely not anything close to OK.

We're here to be OK again. The first step toward okayness is away from willful not-okayness. That means abandoning the things that make you feel not OK.

So just stop it, right? Simple. Ha! If only it were that easy.

What if it could be?

Can you think of ten reasons why you should stop doing what makes you feel not OK?

Yet it's not enough. Those reasons aren't enough alone. Are they? Should and should not are not enough. If shoulds were sufficient, you'd be doing TEDx's. You'd be that counselor who speaks accurately and persuades no one. You'd share that look because you'd know shoulds are empty, futile, and paradoxically worse than silence.

Personal development author Scott Adams writes about the difference between wanting and deciding.[1] I wanted to stop, but I hadn't

---

[1] - Scott Adams, *How to Fail at Almost Everything and Still Win Big: Kind of the Story of My Life*, 2nd ed. (Pleasanton CA: Scott Adams Inc., 2023), 57.

decided. Therein lies my problem: I wanted not to do something. I didn't want something else in its place. I was running in place and chasing the mirage of wanting. Wanting defined me. It was my beginning and my end—my prison.

Wanting is the wish for a solution outside ourselves. Deciding is all within. Deciding is agency. Deciding is the proclamation of I AM and the only start to real change.

It took five weeklong detoxes to reveal to myself what I wanted, not what I didn't want. I wanted to feel normal. In pursuit of normal, I lied to myself. I felt shame and denial. I couldn't admit for so long how not OK I was making myself. To do so would be to admit failure and have no other choice but to accept it as that—failure. It was easier to want to feel like I could be normal again, for a little while, as I did my thing. I feel normal during it. I feel worse after. Shame and denial are unpaused; I do it and feel normal again, then I pause the shame and denial. It went on like this for many years—detoxing on and off again for four years but struggling for a total of eight years. It was a significant amount of not-okayness and an infinite battle.

I was deep in a whirlpool of my own making, a feedback loop that reinforced itself. To be relieved of shame and suffering only required normalcy. I just had to travel back in time and undo my suffering by reversing my reality while leaning into the one experience that guaranteed a singular result: another revolution around the pool.

And so I had to decide. I had to not want anymore. I wanted to feel normal again. I wanted to feel actually normal, not pausing and unpausing, swapping the feeling of normal with shame/denial, over and over, on again off again. I came to realize that I had decided. My life had been an infinite loop of one hour of *this is amazing* with twenty-three hours of *this fucking sucks* every day for weeks, months, years.

The last time I went too far after another long weekend, I woke up on Monday morning feeling surprisingly decent. Then, as I made breakfast, my blood pressure ramped. I knew what that meant. I knew I would have to drink— or soon seek medical help. My stomach lurched as my terror rose. Deciding meant coming clean, bringing my shame into the light and no longer denying it to myself or to others. Deciding meant facing the truth. And so I decided. I couldn't not be OK anymore. It was too systemically painful. I felt like shit every day. I felt guilty every day.

Struggling with my fear, I called my boys, saw my ex-wife, and admitted to them all: I had made the phone call. It was done. I was going to rehab. I had been bathing in shame without lasting change for the better part of a decade. And calling it what it is to those closest to you is what, counterintuitively, allows you to get up and out.

Let me say that again: That which I feared most was also my gateway out. Leaning into exactly what was happening to me, facing head-on the terrible facts that made up my life, offered the real opportunity for change.

This is the surrender you may have heard of. This is the quiet acceptance of reality that opens the hidden door to a new choice.

Remember *The Lord of the Rings*? Gollum, specifically, and his holding on to the ring? That's what it's like to hold on to shame and denial. Doing the thing that makes you not OK and continuing to do it, even while knowing how bad it makes you feel but protecting yourself by keeping the shame hidden. In so doing, you are also keeping out the enthusiastic support. It took me hearing *You are so brave* twenty to thirty times during and after I returned from rehab to believe it. I realized . . . they meant it. These weren't just kind words given to encourage hope. It was real now. Shame went from being like a cloud in a jar to being released and evaporated. And it's another matter, releasing self-hate and receiving the love of others in its place. Facing the decision to stop doing the thing that makes you not OK feels as not OK as anything else ever. Facing the choice feels damn near impossible and far worse than how bad you feel trying to not do the thing that you otherwise liked.

True courage was to admit failure and face defeat. True courage was to lay my shame, my soul, at the feet of loved ones and strangers. What I thought would break me instead set me free.

Yet this is real self-love. It's not getting a massage or telling yourself nice things. Self-love is facing your shame and replacing it with self-compassion. This is another guru word. What the hell does it mean? You have to feel it to

CHAPTER 2 - NORMAL AGAIN

know it. Yet this self-love, this self-care, is waiting inside you.

One unexpected reward? The world is there to support and encourage you. This is in stark contrast to the wanting you to be better than you felt before, dripping with shoulds and judgment.

Everyone knows when you have decided.

Let's look at this one more time. The world knew you were hiding. You lied and protected your Gollum shame like a gift from God. Yet you knew they knew. And the flip side is that the same world around you knows clearly when you've decided you'll accept nothing else other than finding your way through.

That support is waiting within and around you.

And then when you stop doing what makes you not OK, you realize it's going to be OK. It doesn't feel OK. I did not feel OK in rehab for those thirty days of isolation, trust me. But I realized there in my self-imposed locked-in state that the state of not-okayness I had flung myself into every day for nearly a decade just to feel normal again for an hour was not who I was. I *knew* that. And yes, my physiology was adjusting via forced cold turkey feeding. That's what rehabilitation is; it's an extended detoxing. But it wasn't just for my body but also for my mind and my heart. All that I was not, I began to let go of. That wasn't me anymore. It never had been.

So I didn't need to go back. My mask was off, and I didn't have to wear it again because I had let those closest to me see my face for the first time. There's no desire to go back. There's no need to hide. There's no reason to wear the mask again. The mask is known. I'm free.

Free for what? I'd learned who I wasn't, and now I was free to find out who I was. You can be too. I'll explain what I mean shortly.

At this point, I am pretty sure it is past obvious that my thing for that decade was alcohol. I left that detail out of the story because it could be anything for anyone else. My story is a template of all these stories. Yours could be drinking, or it could be sex, food, drugs, screens. It could be working. It could be anything.

My journey on the stage to okayness begins the same as yours will. It's a struggle. First, it's a struggle with what you don't want to feel. Then it's a struggle with what you do want to feel instead. Then it's realizing that whatever your form of escape is, it will never make you feel OK in a lasting way. That this strategy of abusing your thing (and yes, you are, you know you are, don't deny it, we're past that, put the mask down, it's OK) makes you feel better but worse afterward and even worse feeding the loop again. That's when you want to decide. And then something happens when you do decide. That moment for me was the hardest of my life: telling my boys the truth of my shame in the presence of their mother, my ex-wife. You can't skip that; it's the moment of facing the totality of your shame and admitting to all that previous denial.

What brought you to this, and what started it all, may not be your fault, but it damn well is your responsibility.

Others can help you stand temporarily. Or clean you up. Or save you from yourself for a day. Or throw cold water on you. Or try walking away hoping you'll change. Or despairing and bawling with loss. But not a single other person can bring you to a *decision*.

I want you to know that there is a gift in that moment. It's not just that the shame then begins to fade. There's a strength that reveals itself, as that which does not kill you makes you stronger. (I wasn't kidding; there's truth in the trite.) There is no obstacle before or since that compares with that moment of revelation. A truth of who I truly am was revealed. It was like discovering I could deadlift five hundred pounds. (Narrator: He cannot deadlift five hundred pounds.)

I hesitate to encourage you to act now because so many professionals have tried to help me and others stop. And it didn't work. I can't say I have something wise to tell you, wiser than what they said. What I can tell you is that the moment you do decide, you'll feel like you've just walked through a one-way door into something new. Until then, you're stumbling in circles.

All help is self-help. Going to see somebody, checking into rehab, being honest with yourself. That means there will be no more stupid rules you attempt to force upon yourself. "I'm not going to do any more than ____." That's wanting. That's creating another line to cross, requiring force of will that eventually runs out. That's pure hope and not deciding to stop. It's deciding to continue but even more dysfunctionally.

CHAPTER 2 - NORMAL AGAIN

If you can't decide to stop, can you be honest with someone you trust? Bring shame into the light; banish denial. You never know if you're being honest with yourself unless you're telling the truth to someone else. Otherwise, you're just tying yourself in knots. Therapy gets a lot of flak these days, but you need a place to speak freely and be authentic. This requires humility, to admit you need that. Then speak with as much honesty as you possibly can, leaving no lie left untold, instead replaced with truth.

As long as you continue to avoid deciding, I can guarantee there's a lie you're hiding. The shame is distanced from the world by this lie. And in this world of buried lies, every day that you wish for things that aren't true is another day you've decided to remain in your suffering.

All this is building toward the moment of decision, with your agency renewed. The only way out is through, but I have seen rock-bottom moments not work. The only actual rock bottom is death, which is too late, obviously. Nothing makes you want to decide until you do. It's an inner choice, not an outward force. It's inner vulnerability and release of shame. Shame, when felt and admitted, is the strongest motivator. That's when it can't get any worse. Shame is the unavoidable call to action. Because it accelerates self-hate to the point that you can no longer be who you've been, or you will die. Literally. Early on in our work, my therapist (more on my therapy journey soon) told me, "Mark, obviously you want to die." I needed to hear that. Shame is the final state, before death itself. I realized I was on the road to the grave, and it was that emotion that U-turned me.

Shame set me free. Shame was a mentor; I was guided by it away from that willful not-okayness. The only way out of shame is through it, to paraphrase. For me, and for you as well, most likely, the only way to feel normal again is to feel ashamed of yourself. Because of things done to make yourself not OK. And it's OK to feel ashamed of that. That is when you will change. If you're ready, you'll know, and then you'll accept it. Not run from it. *Deny it? Lie?* No. *Change.* Tell the truth, unbottle the shame, and be free. Not quite free to be you yet. Not quite. We'll get there. But right now, you are free to stop. Stop being who you're not.

CHAPTER 2 - NORMAL AGAIN

Be free.

CHAPTER 3

THE ORIGIN STORY OF WHO YOU'RE NOT

What is the son but an extension of the father?
— Frank Herbert, *Dune*

How do we become the person we're not? If you're reading this, there's a damn good chance it has to do with your father. My story does.

There's a certain type of man in Silicon Valley, the type A's type A. He's obsessive and driven, always pushing his limits and those of everyone around him. Nothing is good enough. One hundred percent? Make it 200 percent. A fifty-hour workweek? No, make it eighty. Minimum. You sleep at the office. All meals are work meals. There is no line between work and play. There are no weekends. And a laptop is always within reach.

Why are we this way? Because we were made to be.

Working in the Bay Area, I learned that the tyrannical father is shared by many driven, possessed souls. Every story is as unique as the men who lived them. But the pain is eerily similar, and the healing is equally possible. It didn't feel that way for years. Decades. We stay busy, running from the hurt, hiding the shame and self-loathing. Even the *hate* we have for our parents, for Dad. A short childhood that felt miserably long festers into adulthood. The hurt kid becomes a man himself. But he becomes someone he's *not* to make up for the kid he *had* to be—but shouldn't have to have been—just to feel safe. Usually, no matter what we tried, that feeling evaded us. We longed for it nonetheless.

CHAPTER 3 - THE ORIGIN STORY OF WHO YOU'RE NOT

My struggle was with isolation, in isolation. There's an ocean of difference between being alone and being lonely. For me, the former drove the latter. My father is an only child. My mother was restrained, an introvert. Both had few friends and no guests. We barely saw grandparents, and we never saw cousins. Dad didn't socialize; I learned early on not to bring my own friends over. When he didn't make them feel awkward, he made them feel unwelcome or worse, like he assumed they were an active bad influence in my life. So either I spent Saturday afternoon at my friend's house, or I went without.

Everything ran like clockwork. Home by nine in ninth grade. By ten in tenth grade. By eleven in eleventh grade. Rules for everything. Getting grounded when I broke them. *Can I borrow the car today? No. You borrowed it yesterday. You're grounded. I'm going to go see my friends. No, you're not. You didn't ask first. You're grounded.* It was like being locked in solitary confinement when I was already the only inmate in the whole prison. (I have two younger sisters, four years younger and ten years younger, and it felt like they were over in the women's penitentiary.)

Alone, playing by myself. Alone, head down doing homework. Alone, quiet, next to my sisters. Grounded alone. Eating alone. Hiding alone.

The worst of it was sitting on my hands, on eggshells, by myself. Waiting for the other shoe to drop. Or the hammer. Pick your metaphor. Or all of them. Waiting for the dreaded, *Maaarrrk! What was that?* Or worse, *Maaaarrrk! Come to my office.* Quiet, isolated dread wasn't a story I told myself; it was the atmosphere. It's the intake through osmosis within a family that some therapists refer to as toxic ground. The fear, never spoken of, and the constant vigilance, both become part of you.

That vigilance was the worst. I remember the constant, outward focus. The growing fear. His presence looming out of eyesight. My deep insistence that this time I'd avoid the axe: *I wasn't a bad person.* I kept myself on track. *Not again. I'll do even better. He will see how good I am.* And then the crushing loss, the shame. The look-what-you're-making-me-do judgment. Then the sentence. The isolation. The dark. *The failure.* My God! The constant, unavoidable failure. And the negotiating within the dark emptiness, of the

CHAPTER 3 - THE ORIGIN STORY OF WHO YOU'RE NOT

certainty that there is something wrong with me. I was so not OK.

No longer just a skill, the vigilance melts into your bones and into the earth. Vigilance becomes who you are and a requirement for life around you. It's not a skill; it's a law of nature.

As I grew into my teens, I got my senses. I became aware. An independent self, finally. And with that, growing defiance. And soon, conflict.

• • • •

Let me tell you about the day I orphaned myself. I was eleven. My parents had another argument. About the last move. Career change. *Life* change. Nobody was happy. It was a marriage of two people unhappy alone and even unhappier together. I cowered in my room. Booming voices. Angrier and angrier. Then a pregnant quiet. *Thud, thud, thud, thud* toward my bedroom. My door flew open and bashed the wall.

Mom? I expected Dad.

"Mark?" she said, sounding desperate. Intense. Terrified. "Do you think I should divorce your father?"

I was shocked. Thrilled. *Are you kidding me?* I thought. YES! For a brief moment, a dream I held hidden deep inside burst into light and color. For a moment, I felt the hope of a wildly new future.

Then flinching terror. Disgust. Hate. *How dare you wish your father gone?* And: *How dare you ask your own child that?*

But then I said something different. Out of somewhere and nowhere, words tumbled out.

"That's not for me to decide."

She turned and left and that was it.

I felt like I'd just damned us all. I felt grief for the life I felt for just a moment, waiting beyond her question. But it wasn't my job to tell my mom what to do; it wasn't hers to ask. I felt ashamed for wanting to tell her, "Yes. YES, yes!" I felt powerless for refusing to give that answer. I felt fury at the impossibility of her question. Fury for the magnitude of her fear. And fury for her inability to act on her own. HOW DARE YOU.

After that, I treated neither the same way ever again. The part of me that was determined to prove my father wrong fell into an acceptance of the war between us. And I lost all respect for my mother afterward. Without words, the part

CHAPTER 3 - THE ORIGIN STORY OF WHO YOU'RE NOT

of me that looked to her for solace and comfort and protection gave up on her in that instant. I was a boy without a mom and dad. I watched the clock as I served my time until my sentence was complete.

It wouldn't be until much later in life that I grew to understand my father, especially as he suffered, mellowed, and healed. A story for another time. The point is, as men, we don't turn it up to eleven in all areas of life because we just are that way. We're *made* that way. Shaped. Forced, even. And our defenses are useful, motivating, and profitable. Until they are not. Then we lose what really matters, and we can't buy it back.

Why? Because all we ever wanted was to feel Dad's love.

Why? WHY? I screamed. You screamed. We wanted his approval, or at least acceptance. But we didn't get it.

What's wrong with me? And so that fundamental need of childhood remains long after. Invalidation haunts us.

Something's wrong with me. So we work to prove that thought, feeling, realization wrong. We need to be seen. Get noticed. Command attention. Be a real person worthy of understanding, patience, and respect.

See? The world sees me! See me! Not someone to be manipulated and kept in line. We didn't want a Hallmark card; we wanted a gut-instinct feeling that Dad liked us, rooted for us, maybe even applauded us. He didn't.

What's wrong with me? And so we become someone we're not to make up for the certain failure of the one we are convinced we are—because if we were good enough by default, wouldn't Dad have made that clear? We remain certain of one thing: We are not OK. Not inwardly. So we have to force it outwardly. We must assert control. The outside world must applaud to drown the voices on the inside.

Dad rejected me. He was wrong. I'll show him. That effort began long before I left home. Before I was even an adult. A teenager.

My father's only child status brought an isolation that pervaded his life. Growing up in this pervasive isolation, I was all my dad had at home to relate to or, really, to be controlled by him. So I had to be the best. For him. I tried to get the world's applause; that way, he would hear someone cheer and maybe he would too. That would mean I was OK. I got attention from strangers as I excelled in academia. Praise set the loneliness at bay for decades. As a boy, then as an adult. Then as an entrepreneur. But the short-term glow of external validation could not give me what I needed deeper down. I knew I was not OK, but for years I didn't know why or what to do about it.

It's probably no surprise to you (it was to me) that parental rejection is associated with grave feelings of guilt, shame, and self-consciousness; you feel terrible about yourself, *and* you feel like everyone is watching you, at all times. It's a double whammy. Two ways to lose, no ways to win. Researchers call this an anxious attachment style, which exacerbates "feelings of nonacceptance and distrust," not just with Dad but with everyone close to you.[2]

This comports with my own experience; I wanted Dad's approval, so I threw myself into school, hoping he would finally accept me. It's

---

[2] - Marius Marici, Otilia Clipa, Remus Runcan, and Loredana Pîrghie, "Is Rejection, Parental Abandonment or Neglect a Trigger for Higher Perceived Shame and Guilt in Adolescents?," *Healthcare* 11, no. 12 (2023): 1724, https://doi.org/10.3390/healthcare11121724.

easy to see how you can end up wearing a social mask—and becoming one with it. Becoming this character of not-you. You don't want to feel guilty or ashamed or alone, so you try to do the right thing by putting up an image that others would approve of. The external validation is confirmation that you're all right. So, for a time, the inner turmoil slows because you're not doing anything wrong, at least not in that particular moment. It's not rejection, but it's not approval or acceptance either. More like a low-intensity negative acknowledgment, a feeling of, *Oh. It's you*, coming from one or both parents. But what that little boy needs—unconditional love of both parents but particularly Dad's—he doesn't get. And that laid out the path that ultimately brought you to this book and this chapter and this sentence.

Didn't it?

You're seeking validation because you want the love of your parents—and your father is the biggest challenge to get this validation out of. You try to solve the world using your wounded ego and not your heart. You want other people to tell you that you're OK because you don't feel OK on the inside. You want everyone to tell you

CHAPTER 3 - THE ORIGIN STORY OF WHO YOU'RE NOT

that the mask you wear, the persona you cultivate, is beautiful. Successful. Worthy of acceptance.

Ultimately, this comes from a childish mindset. I'll explain. Children and young adults come up with a great defense strategy to deal with this lack of validation—an OK mindset. This child or young adult wants to be seen as OK to get the love of Dad. When the child or young adult performs, people applaud the facade the child puts up, not the hurting person behind it.

I dealt with the issue by throwing myself into my schoolwork. One way my father attempted to bond with me was by teaching me algebra when I was eight. He thought that I didn't have enough to do during the summer break, and because both my parents were Ph.D.s, my dad made sure I got top grades. Do well in elementary school because it gives you the tools for middle school; do well in middle school because it gives you the tools for high school; do well in high school because it gives you the tools for college. I got straight As so that I could stay valuable; it became my identity.

This behavior extended to college. That was a new beginning for me, so I wanted to enjoy the experience. I desperately needed something to balance how hard I knew I would work. I chose the University of Virginia because it had the reputation of being a party school, and I didn't want to go into ROTC as would be required at my out-of-state choices. I was baptized into its party culture, which helped me be more open; I wasn't this tortured kid anymore. Living in that dorm felt a bit freer, and the best part was that no one criticized being smart or working hard, so I still had that going for me. It was a work hard, play hard sort of thing. Feel free to get your T-shirt at Mincer's stating so. My dad always told me to treat school like a job from Monday to Friday, and I did that. But on the weekends? I made friends. I met women. I binge drank. I took full advantage of the broad and diverse social environment that college offered me.

That freedom gave me space to explore something inside me. I could focus more on projecting myself outward instead of nursing inner wounds from a lack of validation. Still, all that repression at home left its crater in me. Much like an elephant that remains tied to a stake because it was taught powerlessness from birth, I still didn't feel

CHAPTER 3 - THE ORIGIN STORY OF WHO YOU'RE NOT

free to validate myself internally, instead choosing to validate externally.

I joined the accelerated master's program and graduated into a stalled economy. With job prospects mixed at best, I went for a Ph.D. But that didn't work out either. I ended up settling into a small software company in Silicon Valley; lucky for me, I realized it was the best time in my life to do something risky.

There I found I was atypically risk tolerant. Although I didn't seek out risks, I took opportunities when they came, even if they were ones others passed on. I looked for asymmetric opportunities, like any other entrepreneur. I didn't get paid much at first, but that was OK because my financial world was just me, for a while (the equation changed with a wife and kids). Thus, I fully embraced the type A within.

And it worked. It worked better than business school could have. My business partner and best friend, Sanjay, hadn't studied business either. You can probably guess how the story went: A few guys chased a dream, working for long hours and low (or no) pay, developing a software product that could become the next big (enough) thing. And we made it. A valuable business acquired.

We had *decided* failure was not an option. We were driven to make this work at any cost. And we did. But *how* we did it should have, at the time, made me realize I was not the person I'd thought myself to be.

At home as a child, it was forbidden to be yourself. Only strict adherence to the rules was allowed. Actions required permission; speech required due care. Yet, unexpectedly, I dropped that with Sanjay and our other leaders. We made a commitment to be honest about the state of *everything*. We were transparent about how anything and everything was going at all times. We'd get deep into brainstorming sessions and lose our egos amid the ideas. No issue was fatal; there was always a way. We trusted one another so much that I was able to lose my mask and embrace the truth of each work situation. Amid the chaos of start-up life, I was half OK. Or at least better, with authentic action front and center and my pain distant and buried.

The storm was my calm. Actual adversity, like bootstrapping a business during the most

CHAPTER 3 - THE ORIGIN STORY OF WHO YOU'RE NOT

competitive period of Silicon Valley history, made me feel safe. It was at this point that I realized that I was more than my mask. Pieces of the true me revealed themselves. Although the external world defined what success was (as it always is in business), I saw me for me for the first time I can remember.

Soon, the company went from failing to not failing to *dominating*. My personal life mirrored my business life, with marriage, children, and our home. There were challenges, obstacles, and peace despite turbulence. But beneath it all was a wounded little boy who had addressed nothing. The type A kept pushing, going, moving, driving, crushing, succeeding.

It was only when I had to sit still again that I came undone. I could no longer be who I was not. Leaving the Bay Area and moving to Lake Tahoe after a successful exit from the software business, my mask had no more use—not to anyone else, and not to me.

That's when my marriage imploded and when my drinking went from moderate and social to abusive and excessive. There was no other way.

To an outside observer, I was living the dream. I had enough money to retire at forty—that's how well I was doing. But even so, I was convinced that there was something wrong with me, and that feeling didn't go away. In fact, it intensified. After taking several walks alone with my own thoughts, I realized that I didn't like living this life. I didn't like living full-time in Tahoe. I didn't like going from a driven type A to a despondent type Z. Most of what I thought was important no longer was.

The divorce was going forward, whether I liked it or not. I hated the reality that my kids would soon be the children of divorce, but here I was. Part of my mask was that there was no way—no *way*—that I was the type of person who got divorced, yet here I am. The divorce was my worst personal failure, and it wounded my children in a way that I could not accept. From a very early stage in our marriage, we told each other that divorce was not an option. With every disagreement, with every argument, even as the tension rose, we told each other this.

None of this helped, because we weren't addressing the cracks in the foundation of our

CHAPTER 3 - THE ORIGIN STORY OF WHO YOU'RE NOT

marriage. Instead of fixing these cracks, we were strengthening our mutual denial and arguing about bullshit on the surface. So when it blew apart, it did so in a huge way. We focused on what we didn't want instead of on what we did want, so there was no unifying purpose, no mission. When the marriage fell apart, I fell apart too.

All this was because I refused to take off my mask of delusion. I held on to that delusion for dear life because of how it looked to other people, how it protected me. It was the mask of insecurity I wore because of that unhealed parental acceptance wound. Whenever you have these beliefs about what you should not do, about what's not acceptable, about what you're not, that's a tell for what your mask is portraying to the world. You're more worried about how you'll look if unacceptable things did happen. You refuse to accept that which is.

That's the definition of suffering. It was at that point when my drinking went from (heavy) social to toxic—I was trying to keep the state of denial afloat until I couldn't do so any longer. I had to take the mask off. The universe had spoken, and I had to listen. Had I faced the truth years earlier, my marriage might have been saved, and my sons would have gone through far less wounding.

This may be the case for you. You may be seeing parts of my story cast shadows on yours. The details are different; the feelings are identical. Even now, you may be having several aha moments, knowing how you got the way you are not. The mask may be useful. It may serve many purposes for your station in life, in business, and in both. But consider what happens when the status quo is disrupted. The love-hate relationship with the mask loses the love. It's a paradox that becomes all pain. Then the only way out of it is through it. Put this process off, and it may be too late to do what you could have done, to be who you might have been. It's never too late to do the right thing, but relationships can have expiration dates if not prioritized and nurtured. Save yourself the pain. You don't do yourself any favors by putting up false fronts and *keeping* them up with those closest to you. I sometimes wonder how things would have gone in my marriage if I'd brought the entrepreneurial honesty of my professional work to my ex over the true

CHAPTER 3 - THE ORIGIN STORY OF WHO YOU'RE NOT

state of myself and our marriage. How different things would be now. How little I would have needed, or even wanted, alcohol.

I may wonder how different it would have been, but I have absolute clarity about one truth: pure honesty was coming one way or the other. Sooner would have allowed far more potential for healing with my ex and for reduction of harm with my sons. I'd give my right arm, if I could, to give that a shot.

The way our fathers treat us is not our fault; the man we're shaped to be isn't either. But now we get the chance to reshape ourselves. That is our responsibility and our *gift*. This is a tangible meaning of life being a journey, not a destination. The good news is that the drive to succeed grants more resources in the face of difficulty; the bad news is that we can drive ourselves into ruin. We're on the hamster wheel until we're not, and we collapse.

Wherever you are on this journey, mask still on or mask freshly off, facing your true self comes with a universal consequence: You'll need to forgive yourself. Self-mercy is so great a feat to complete that, in spite of everything, it's easier to slide the mask back on and go about the rest of your life being who you know you're not.

Forgiving your father is hard. Forgiving yourself is harder.

I hope you're up for the challenge.

CHAPTER 4

FORGIVING THE MAN YOU WEREN'T

The weak can never forgive. Forgiveness is the attribute of the strong.
—Mahatma Gandhi

How can you forgive yourself? Slowly, then suddenly.
We are all foolish beings. Another trite and true statement. I puzzled on that one for years. I first heard this from a spiritual teacher I greatly respect. He says it often. I didn't get it. Then, one

day, I did. When finally I unraveled the meaning of it all, this is what I realized: I needed to forgive myself. For being who I was and doing what I did all those years without knowing any better. You see, there's no owner's manual for being a human. And especially not when you're a kid.

We discover ourselves as children with no idea of how we got there or why. Or how to do it. We are innocent and terribly vulnerable. Then our parents screw us up. (Be careful when you become one, and also be ready for repair.) In addition, our tribe, schools, culture, extended family, friends—all of them mold us, wound us, and poison us, regardless of intention. In response, our childhood selves hide those scars we can't deal with. The psyche has to protect the wound. We bury it. *I won't let that happen again.* And: *STAY OUT.* We wrap up the sins of others in armor and with energy, and we mount defenses that proclaim *NEVER AGAIN*.

Later in life, you realize what you've done. To yourself. Sometimes in therapy, other times with a spiritual teacher, or just on a walk alone in the woods with your cell phone off, you see what you've done. You wake up in a labyrinth

CHAPTER 4 - FORGIVING THE MAN YOU WEREN'T

of your own making, wearing a mask that's not you. A maze and a mess of your choices, your consequences, and others' choices and their consequences. It's like in the story of Theseus and the Minotaur when the hero of the story used a golden thread to find his way into the great prison-maze of the beast—and then back out. Except there's no thread, and you have no sword to defend yourself from the monsters of the past. It's terrifying, and yet it's a gift. It took me more than fifteen years to see it that way. The gift of riding a bicycle comes with taking off the training wheels. To wake up is to no longer be asleep, wandering around clueless as to who you are and why you do as you do.

We are foolish beings, wounded without consent. The story of how and why is told beneath the surface of your daily conscious awareness; it's an invisible script. Now you know that. So you have your agency, for the first time in a long time. And that gives us a job to do—get out of jail. Forgiveness of self is the key. I didn't make the connection until, again, one day I just finally did.

This is the challenge: The you-now is challenged to forgive the you-then. That version of you who was lost in the maze, buried in the past, refused to change. And you know what consequences *those* choices brought you. That's hard to admit, but the sooner you do, the sooner you get to what's next: to realize that the you-then was not you. The you-now is more you. That person back then with those parents in that environment and through those dark times did the best he could. He was a kid who knew no better, but then he became an adult, and now he does. Facing this truth is the way out. The task now is to forgive. You, like me before you, probably struggle to forgive this not-you who you were.

Here's how I let go of the suffering and the judgments: I embraced responsibility. I did this first with my sons, asking myself, *How can I best be there for them now?* I also did this with my friends, asking, *How can I mend my rifts with them?* Eleven-year-old me wasn't really in charge of his own life. So I can forgive that little guy for deciding between shitty choices. I don't need arrogance—that is, that false inner knowing that *I should have done it right the first time;*

CHAPTER 4 - FORGIVING THE MAN YOU WEREN'T

I should have known better. Seeing my loved ones for who they are enabled me to switch that same compassion lens to myself. THAT helped.

Still, it's tempting to look away and into another lens, not that of compassion but of *comparison*. So tempting. It doesn't seem like others with their flawless Instagram lives suffer from any of this. Their lives are perfect, right? No, not really. Everyone is messed up. Every. One. Everyone is living a life of quiet desperation. You think other men have it all together? They do until they don't, and you may not know it.

Economist Thomas Sowell once said, "There are no solutions, only trade-offs." This is the trade-off of the mask we've worn: We could either *look* great for social media and the world at large, or we could *be* great for ourselves. We didn't make this trade-off (in the unhelpful direction) consciously, not most of us. It *feels* right because it's the validation of the mask. That's why we wear it so long after it was useful in childhood, when being someone we weren't helped keep us safe.

There was this one guy I knew. At the time, he had recently turned forty. He was at my sister's wedding, catching up with friends he hadn't seen in a while. I overheard everyone who hadn't seen him for so long tell him how good he looked. I knew he wanted to believe it. But I'd seen him on and off more recently. I happened to notice he'd been putting on weight. He once remarked offhand that his pants didn't feel the same. The women in particular were the worst about it—saying what would make him feel good, even when it clearly wasn't true. I took my old friend aside and shot straight: *Do not listen to anyone who says you look fine. You know in your heart and in your gut. If you think you're getting fat, go to the gym and keep going. Never listen to pretty lies.*

This is what we do to put off the dirty job of necessary self-forgiveness. We keep on the squeaky-clean mask of a perfect life, as best we can. We're not in a good place, but we try to appear as if we are so that we can get the praise that we never received in our young life when we needed it most. But then when we *did* succeed and things *were* going our way, the unconscious urgency subsided.

CHAPTER 4 - FORGIVING THE MAN YOU WEREN'T

I lived the life of praise for my mask. I had the beautiful wife. I had the sweet kids. I had the company du jour. We were ready to go public. The market conditions were strong; our company was a leader in technology that our broader sector needed badly. Buoyed by this life-changing windfall, my then-wife advised that we should reflect for a year on our new potential and not do anything crazy except go on one really nice vacation. (This was great advice for anyone who suddenly has a lot more money. Patience breeds perspective.)

Then we chose to relocate to Lake Tahoe and live quieter, slower-paced lives. We had family all over the West Coast, and we had spent tons of time in Tahoe. We talked to the locals and cleared all of our questions. An already fairy-tale existence turned into an even bigger fairy tale. I was living the dream.

Then everything fell apart.

It wasn't just the alcoholism. My marriage fell apart as my past came alive now that the hustle and demands of leadership were gone. I tried a million different ways to live a different life in Tahoe, far from Silicon Valley. I watched friends become venture capitalists and make millions upon millions of dollars and start new companies. Though I helped with some of these start-ups, I couldn't get too involved because I didn't live down there. And I didn't want to just spend my life doing technology. I didn't want to chain myself to the hamster wheel of start-ups and whatnot. I wanted to figure out what life was without that defining me. I thought I was putting my family first, but the opposite occurred—it tore us apart.

In my mind, I was being punished for doing a good thing. Whether from the divorce, from moving away, or from something else, so many options were closed to me now. Because of this, some of it due to my own decisions, I spiraled into addiction. I was so far gone into the labyrinth that it wasn't until I realized that was the case that I had any hope of escape.

As the sum total of my failure dawned on me, I sank deeper into despair. We can't turn back the clock, so we're stuck with the decisions we already made and the lifespan we have left. Everything's either a positive feedback loop with success compounding upon success or a negative

CHAPTER 4 - FORGIVING THE MAN YOU WEREN'T

feedback loop with failure compounding upon failure. Despair is the negative feedback loop on full power; I felt shut out of opportunities, shut out of life.

Life became punishment. And I was certain I was guilty.

If you're also suffering in this way, telling you to just forgive yourself is pretty damn useless. But forgiveness is a muscle. It can be developed. The easiest way to do this is to work on forgiving others. Community. Support. Group therapy. You will absolutely swim in compassion for what has happened to others, even for what they did to themselves *just as you did*. Not sure how to forgive? Sit with someone tearing themselves slowly, precisely to pieces. You will build that muscle so fast that you'll be rippling with self-compassion.

Like physical fitness, this work takes time. I went through a four-year self-development program, and one of the final things we did was practice deep healing around self-forgiveness. And we did have to practice; it was shocking to watch people who spent years sharing their pain then struggle with forgiving themselves. This isn't something you can do just by reading about it in a book—you have to do it actively.

One facet Alcoholics Anonymous (AA) gets right is the sharing of acceptance and personal responsibility. AA may or may not be your cup of tea, but these communal acknowledgments are the wellspring of compassion and forgiveness.

In group sessions, I've heard from every walk of life—ages nineteen to eighty-six, male, female, every religion and none, every job, every aspiration. So many suffered from self-hate far worse than mine, to the point where I thought I was lying to myself about how much I hurt. It was impostor syndrome for my own suffering. *Who was I to offer up compassion when I've never gone through the privations that they did?*

But when the sharing got past the specifics, I heard my pain and my words coming out of others' mouths. This shatters the illusion that you're all alone. It teaches you to forgive someone just like you, which extends to forgiving yourself, specifically the not-you of your own childhood and adolescence. Self-forgiveness is the key, and it unlocks you from the prison of the past. It also grants you a blessing you may find unfamiliar or even unheard of—your own personal agency. It was the compassionate community who helped reveal this.

Love for others, love for self, love for others even more. A positive feedback loop.

In simple terms, *agency* is just you making conscious and deliberate choices, but there's more to it than that, especially when you struggle with forgiving yourself. When you're thinking about things, ask yourself this: *What would a good father do? What would a good mother do? What would a good friend do? Is that thought mine, or is it coming from someone else?* You may make a decision, and that decision may result in failure, but it was *your* decision, and you can make different ones. This is agency. Instead of hiding from failure with a false mask, you push through failure by continuing to do better for yourself and those around you, not from the perfectionism of that old not-you but from a genuine desire to create more of what you want—that is, what *you* want. It's the change from *I really don't want to be drinking so much* to *I want to live in the moment fully with my family and remember this for the rest of my life*. (This was so essential to my transformation from broken to whole that I'm dedicating the next chapter to it; it's harder than it sounds because you've spent so many years trying *not* to embrace the present moment and all the pain it brings. Anyway, next chapter.)

Note that this agential choice differs from will or willpower. Will is about what you *should* do and what someone else thinks is correct, like your father (yikes, no going back there). Agency, instead, is more about what you are capable of doing and what you can change. Will is the stick, agency is the carrot. What makes this attractive is that the only way to end your suffering is *to change*—that is, to choose. You want the mask-earned suffering to end? Make it end through action; don't just salve it with addiction. And addiction likewise has its opposite—connection. With others. Who get it. Who forgive you. Just as you forgive them. Resulting in gratitude. Which feeds itself.

And finally, you start to feel better. There's hope again. It comes when you're honest with yourself and when you allow yourself to see not only how unhealthy you've been but also how

CHAPTER 4 - FORGIVING THE MAN YOU WEREN'T

much in your life is not going the right way, even if you've been pretty materially comfortable.

The truth will set you free. But first, it stings like a motherfucker. I had so much to feel shame for. My personal failures hurt my boys. I sank into the hell of alcoholism. I lost my marriage. Taken together, I was a shell of who I once was. That was the truth. I had to hit rock bottom, drowning in addiction. This was how I stopped. Rather than being ashamed that I could not control my drinking anymore (sooner or later I'd chug vodka), I admitted defeat and accepted my self-imposed lot in life, the one that was a cascade of events that my eleven-year-old self was ultimately responsible for (though without his initial consent; this is a nuanced topic, which you understand). I gave up my pride, the sense I was all that, and, more importantly, my arrogance, the persistent belief that I *should not* have been who I was or done as I did.

The shoulds that feed the addiction are the exact opposite of forgiveness. They are whips and chains. They are all lies. Should or should not, what happened *happened*.

How did I move on? Other than clear and present dangers to my health, my boys came first. They saw me drink myself into a stupor, and I knew I had to change right then and there. I went to their events. I guilt-bought too many presents. Overall, I ask myself, sometimes daily, What would a healthy father do? And then I do that. I'll also be honest: I am not entirely free of guilt. But I am past the shame.

I realized that failure was a two-way street. My ex and I each had a lot of work to do on ourselves. And, far too late, we both did so. Here's some simple wisdom I gained with the benefit of hindsight: Be proactive on the health of your marriage. Don't accept the tiniest moments of contempt. You can find copious amounts of research on contempt, and it is the death knell.

Forgiveness is both past and present. You have to forgive yourself, but you also have to change using your agency. Again (because I really can't say it enough or overstate its impact), group therapy is ideal for this. Nobody there is masking a perfect life. There's none of this pretending; it's all out in the open, and everyone has to face everything if they want to move past it.

CHAPTER 4 - FORGIVING THE MAN YOU WEREN'T

You go from that hell of self-condemnation to a desire to be your best.

I didn't think of it this way at the time, but I started working my agency muscles early on in the process, a bit more literally. I dieted but kept learning, so my baseline eating kept improving. I moved more, and I found new sports that I took joy in, such as wakesurfing and backpacking. I cut the negativity out of my life, instead seeking out the beautiful things. I made changes that resonated deeper in me. I felt the health in it, the rightness. I felt it in my heart-mind.

How do I live with myself given everything I did while being who I wasn't? Healing is holding it all, the guilt and the desire to forgive myself. Much that happened was awful, and much of it was my fault, but what can I do now?

Up until 2019, my plan was to move backward into normalcy. I was going to detox, then get back into the swing of things. I couldn't do it all at once, so I did it step-by-step. I watched what I ate. I cut alcohol out of my life. I celebrated the small victories, knowing that they would add up to much bigger triumphs. My experience has been revelatory: Who I am is not perfectible and never was. I can accept that.

Our childhoods are full of programming, through both domineering and cultural osmosis. Defenses are built imperfectly by inexperienced and fragile little beings. Addiction develops as a defense mechanism, fueled by culture and often founded in genetics. And we wake up to our madness when we do. Embrace the possibilities and the responsibility and drop the judgment and the arrogance.

You don't have your full agency until you heal the ego—with forgiveness and acceptance of its guilt—and until you acknowledge your perpetual guaranteed imperfection, no matter how hard you wish otherwise. In other words, nobody's perfect, we're never going to be, and that's OK. Understand this, and you understand how to forgive yourself: for who you were then, who you are now, and who you will be—and who you won't be, no matter how hard you try.

Forgive.

CHAPTER 5

RELEASE FROM THE PAST, INTO THE PRESENT

How you do anything is how you do everything.
—Martha Beck

Have you ever read "The Tale of the Golden Spool"? It goes something like this:

A young boy, often impatient with the mundane or unhappy with the challenging moments of life, encounters a witch or a magical figure who offers him a golden ball or spool with a thread coming out of it. The witch explains that by pulling on the thread, he can fast-forward through parts of his life that he doesn't want to experience or that he finds difficult. Eager to avoid discomfort and ready for future happiness, the boy grabs the opportunity.

As he grows, whenever he faces anything unpleasant, difficult, or tedious, such as exams, heartbreak, illness, or even everyday frustrations, he pulls the thread, skipping those moments. However, as he continues to do so, he suddenly finds himself an old man. He realizes that he has missed out on virtually his entire life, including many profound, joyful, and crucial learning experiences. He skipped not only the bad parts but

CHAPTER 5 - RELEASE FROM THE PAST, INTO THE PRESENT

also the good parts that naturally follow life's challenges.

In his old age, filled with regret, he reflects on the life he missed and the experiences he never got to savor. The boy, now an old man, understands too late that the challenging and tedious moments he avoided were integral parts of life's journey. These moments were, in fact, opportunities for personal growth, happiness, and the accumulation of memories and relationships that define the very fabric and vitality of one's life.

The moral of the story is . . . what, exactly? That patience is a virtue? Uh, yeah? Maybe? Or perhaps the moral is if you want to check out from life's dull moments, you might miss the sublime beauty of them? Well, this parable is (or was) often taught to school-age children, and I don't know if they yet comprehend words like *sublime* or the real-world feeling it entails. The parable seems to be teaching that we *should not* long to skip through life. The pain, toil, and suffering. That it is better to endure the bad times than to skip them and enjoy only the good.

That message sucks. Why? Why is it good to feel bad?

This lesson is taught to kids as if it is obviously and elementarily profound. It will serve you in life. OK, how? Why? "Just be present in every moment because that is good" assumes value in presence alone. I would have liked that old parable (and other teachings like them) to teach us why. Maybe I can help us do that.

Here's what I learned from reflecting on it all—my father, the alcohol, my divorce, and my journey to something like healing with all the pitfalls along the way:

I spent decades avoiding living fully in the moment, trying not to feel what I was experiencing. The suffering lived beyond just the present. It was in the unhealed festering cries of an eleven-year-old. In how I felt the day my son found me passed out on the floor. And in visions of my ex's wounded eyes. All of this, living deep in the pain and the shame.

But my son didn't know. My sons had no knowledge about what happened in my

CHAPTER 5 - RELEASE FROM THE PAST, INTO THE PRESENT

childhood, the one I was running from and drinking so much to escape. By trying *not* to live in the present moment, I wasn't living at all, not in the way those close to me could perceive. To them, I turned into a misty half spirit. And *that* is what that old, dumb fable should have taught us but didn't.

Running away on the inside covered those I loved most in abandonment.

It is noble to live in the moment, in every moment. Me not being present in *my* present moment meant I could not be present for my son in *his* present moment. The more we live in the present moment, the easier it gets—and the less we feel an urge to escape it. We feel less an urge to escape it when we have faced the monsters hiding in our closets. We can rest comfortably with the one wounded from being asked if his parents should divorce, from the one deeply ashamed when confronted to evict his girlfriend from staying for dinner, from the one hiding under covers in terror while arguments pounded on the other side of the wall. We sit with what was once a cacophony, now transmuted with all those pieces returned home. So bring them home, with each moment. *Be* in the moment of the present so that the past may fade as an influence in your day-to-day, each day.

Want to be fully in the moment? Watch the sunrise. Have sex. Jump out of a plane. Go to the gun range. These can be great avenues for being present. They can be escapes. Or they can help point the way. Engaged in these activities, you are not mulling the past. You are not anxious about the future. And I would hope you are fully focused, in two examples at least, because you'll die otherwise. There's also a blatant or hidden beauty in each of these, an invitation or a demand to be fully with what is happening.

But what about the rest of your day, your life? I know you seek solace and find it temporarily.

My story is not unique. Maybe this will ring a bell with you. I abused alcohol (and myself) because I was escaping pain. Running from the trapped emotions of the past. But I also indulged to ease the stress of the future. My wounded self had determined to never allow the same wounds again.

OK, Mark, so just go have fun, is that it? Is that how you heal the broken relationships, the

CHAPTER 5 - RELEASE FROM THE PAST, INTO THE PRESENT

terrible traumas, and the long-suffering misery brought up by yourself and heaped upon others?

Yeah, no. That's trite. Shoot guns, jump out of planes, you'll feel better. *That* is escape. A conscious escape. Enlightenment is waking up to the reality that there's nowhere else to go. Living in the present for yourself and with others takes work. That work, as far as I've been able to tell, takes the form of two jobs: presence to recover from the pain of the past and presence to engage and maintain contact with the present moment (with wisdom to leave the future to the future).

Releasing the negativity, for me, first came through therapy. But even improving your relationship with just yourself works. You're answering the questions like, for example, *Why do I act this way? Why did I yell at my son? Why did that argument with my ex trigger me so extremely?* And you're answering them with patience, sitting with the toughest questions. Resisting the egocentric demand for immediate resolution. Be the journey.

For me, rather than escaping (through alcohol, by literally leaving the house, or obsessing on work), I leaned into the present. What's happening is not going away.

With one of my sons, we struggled with electronics. (Who doesn't?) One week we had family staying with us. It was important to me that we all spent dinner together. My son showed up with his iPhone and was buried in it. We had had days of small skirmishes. That day, I slipped into full battle. I was upset; I felt about him the way my father probably felt about me. I realized this: It wasn't about the phone. It was about blocking out his family and being rude to me in a way I knew my father would never have stood for with me. Rather than acting on my rising anger, I took a deep breath. I got curious. I took him aside one-on-one after dinner and asked him why.

As he recovered from the surprise of encountering compassion instead of anger, he shared with me his own deep sadness. (A private story.) We chose understanding over conflict, such as the kind my father and I had been consumed by for years during my own adolescence. And so we reconnected. It was a real-time moment of realizing that what I had been programmed to be and do in that instant was the younger

CHAPTER 5 - RELEASE FROM THE PAST, INTO THE PRESENT

wounded me; I allowed that version of me, that not-me, to heal—by repairing the connection with my son over the iPhone. What would have remained a low-intensity, taxing, useless, hurtful war in the house for days ended in connection, life-affirming understanding, and closeness. We traded a small useless battle for real connection to hold dear.

Presence, empathy, and connection rather than resistance, escape, and suffering.

After that, when we had dinner as a family, he put his phone down and engaged (most of the time—let's be real). Because I had learned to have the language of connection around the topic. I had been shamed as a youngster; I got to release that shame by ceasing to shame my own son. And transgressions became what they were: small moments that can be easily resolved.

Funny how that works. Living in the present. That's in the repair. Mistakes always happen. Misunderstandings with friends happen. You lean into real honest conversation.

It's the hero's journey, not the hero's destination. My journey became all about small moments leaning into postdrinking repair.

I shared my shame. My remorse. My desire for repair and connection. I told them what I realized was the truth: Connection with each of them was of absolute critical importance. I shared my fear that they would leave home and, like me, have a distant, strained relationship with their father. I talked about therapy and why most people need it. And about the power of speaking honestly.

A lot of this was slowing myself down and facing my emotional landscape—what feelings I'm having, how they feel, what those feelings are called, how those feelings are stirred, and what works through and processes those emotions. Somatic therapy was key (actually feeling my feelings versus living in circuitous labeling and thinking about my feelings). Where does this live in my body? Its shape. Its texture or temperature. Movement. Density. I had held my emotions at bay for decades, ruminating, analyzing my emotions without feeling them so that they stuck around, pooled up like a mucky green slime pond rather than flowing on and through like a crystal clear river so clean you can drink it. Somatic therapy allowed me to make sense

CHAPTER 5 - RELEASE FROM THE PAST, INTO THE PRESENT

particularly of the past; I could see myself and painful moments from the past like Polaroid photos. What happened. What was said. I had run from them. My mind wanted to label those photos "OK, fine, it happened, whatever, just don't think about it" but somatic therapy brought me to relabeling those photos with accurate emotions—what it really was that I felt. Allowing it to be felt and allowing it to be released. It's a little weird to describe, but when you call it what it is, you free it. Your body feels unstuck. That old stale feeling trapped deep inside somewhere lets go and seeps out when you stop lying to yourself about its existence. It's free and so are you. Again, weird. Bizarre. Experiencing what it is, dropping the analysis, is to live in the moment and make peace with the past. Short-term pain; long-term healing.

I swear, each and every truth has this bittersweet combination of being both obvious once experienced and yet almost despairing in this clarity: There was always only this path waiting for each and every one of us. The only way out (say it with me).

I'll emphasize this for a moment. You're probably type A like me. You excel at analyzing and rumination. You are most comfortable in your mind. That mind does not feel; it thinks. Consider how often you think about the past, but you don't feel it. As you open up the pictures of the past, you may well need practice to actually feel what took place. In your body. That is somatic therapy.

I also found a growing presence and peace with meditation. Take the moment my mom asked me if she should divorce my father, with the overwhelming shame I held for wanting her to do exactly that. And my shock. Anger. Terror. And this deep quiet resolution to tell her it wasn't my place to answer. I *knew* what those emotions were as I felt them, but I labeled them with logic and refused to live through them as feelings. I denied them. What it was. How I felt. I didn't want to come to grips with those and other feelings about my parents, especially my father. But no way out but through; not for me, not for you. Give yourself the grace of contemplation. When the memories of the feelings return (and you know they do), allow yourself to sit with them. Why do I resist? What is that feeling telling me? If I could experience that feeling and let it make its peace and pass, how would *that* feel? And now give yourself the grace of patience and presence, and then feel it all. This is best done alone, without distractions like a computer or a phone if you can help it. Self-honesty helps you live with yourself again—in the moment and in moments past. It's further forgiving and cleansing the not-you within.

Meditation can also be found in the smallest of things. Zen that shit. Zen and the Art of Snow Shoveling. Zen and the Art of Cleaning the Kitchen. For me, these both (for real, not joking) became a form of walking meditation. The former I fell into as I exhausted myself after a week of twelve-foot blizzards. The latter, post divorce, was a sense of doing it MY DAMN WAY. (Can I get an amen from the postdivorcées out there?) Each a journey of practicing the skill of being with the present. Of being present. Of being. And each an example of *how you do anything* is *how you do everything*—a truth that stings looking in the rearview mirror.

What about building new, more *positive* experiences so that you can look forward to a distraction-free day? Presence in the present. Well, men, especially, hit the gym. Get tired. When rage and other feelings came for me, I gave myself an alternative: I would hike for hours, bagging peaks with minimal stuff, just water. (I actually scared myself once when I made a wrong turn. Not smart in the boonies of Tahoe. Carry water!) One of the best things I did was walk the Pacific Crest Trail for four hundred miles. I learned salsa and bachata (no, I'm not that great). Wakesurfing. I took singing lessons (and still do).

Exhausting self and mind is a simple path to presence.

Most modern men live sedentary, inactive lives with little sleep—all this together with stress keeps cortisol (the stress hormone) high and endorphins low. There is a biochemical component to living the good life again, without longing to escape everyday moments. Cortisol cooks the brain. You can't be present with your fight-or-flight response activated; your world narrows tightly. In the case of type A guys my age,

CHAPTER 5 - RELEASE FROM THE PAST, INTO THE PRESENT

we're stressed by the past and its consequences in the present. Not alive in the present moment.

Physical effort sets you free to live in the moment. When men get tired physically, we feel better mentally and emotionally. Physical exertion means freedom. Tire ourselves out through physical effort, and we land in a place of clarity. We see things for what they are, with cleaner lenses, less affected by what came before and what blemishes we might have otherwise brought back from the past into the present. We can just *be*. Climb a peak with your buddy, high-five at the top, and you did something with your body that you feel proud of. Your body feels proud of itself, biochemically. Arduous challenges undertaken and accomplished let you live with yourself again because the person you've been living with just did something tremendously hard.

There are only two kinds of feedback loops—negative and positive. This is the easiest positive feedback loop to start. This is where I should tip you off to how I learned about cortisol and the brain—no man is an island, nor is he his own doctor. It was by reaching out to domain experts with credibility in the symptoms I felt, their causes, and the possible solutions that I found practical ways to release the past—and release myself and my thoughts fully into the present.

The past is the past. The present is forever. There will never not be a moment when you live that is not the present moment.

Read that again. Study it. Meditate on it. For that is how to live vibrantly.

CHAPTER 6

EVERY MAN IS AN ISLAND

All healing happens through relationship.
— Myōgen Jason Shulman

I will try anything to see if it works, and if it does, I don't care why.

It is often said that no man is an island—that we are influenced by everything and everyone around us, and through our actions we influence other people and things. Although this may be true, it's not the whole story.

What's also true is that *every* man is an island—when you have to apply your knowledge and change your life, only you can do that. No one can learn for you or improve your life skills for you. No one can eat right for you, and no one can exercise for you. No one can get healthy for you. All of it has to be done with your own effort.

But there's another way in which a man becomes an island—if he doesn't get his life right, he drives everyone else away.

For example, alcohol abuse brings shame, and shame brings isolation, especially from a wife and kids. Getting out of shape makes you physically repulsive. Continued unemployment makes it harder to get a job, and so on. In your broken state, you isolate yourself further from the world, and only your personal efforts can get you out of this state.

But don't think that there's some twelve-step plan I can give you that will take you from broken to healed. The best I can do is offer you guidelines and signposts, with things you must apply to change how your life is going.

You can't boil the ocean. You can't dig a trench with a spoon. But you can turn the negative

CHAPTER 6 - EVERY MAN IS AN ISLAND

feedback loop of bad conditions causing isolation causing worse conditions causing more isolation by building positive feedback loops that make things easier as you go. Don't think of the entire problem all at once. Instead, break it into smaller problems you can solve and habits you can build so that you solve the problem just by doing what you regularly do.

Before we begin with actionable steps, you must understand one thing: Life happens. The world isn't going to pause itself while you try to figure out how to solve your problems. Your business deals will blow up. Your ex will drive you crazy. Friends may pull away because they're tired of your chaos. You might receive a bill you didn't know was coming. Much will happen as you sort things out, so brace yourself for that.

How, Mark?

Get the right people on your team. Take care of yourself. Here's where I suggest you start.

The first thing you'll need, and you won't believe this, is a therapist. Take it from me; it's impossible to move forward from this personal darkness without the aid of a good therapist.

Later in this chapter, I'll lay out how to find a good fit. But as you may assume, you need more than just the therapist; you need other people you can speak honestly with, be it a circle of good friends, a trusted family member, or others. On top of that, you need a community. This may contradict the idea of you being an island, but remember, all those people can't improve yourself for you. You have to take what they share and change it into action.

Then have your brain checked out, whether by a psychiatrist or through MRIs and such—whichever you can afford. Before you can solve why you're not OK, you need to know if something is wrong with you in the first place, beyond sadness about your current situation.

You'll be assessed with cognitive tests, and they'll look at your therapeutic history. They'll assess your emotions. From here, you'll learn if you have any underlying mental issues, such as anxiety or depression. When I went through it, I was in the top 4 percent on anxiety and the top 20 percent on depression. This latter result didn't surprise me; I was in the middle of a depressive episode when I got there. These assessments

CHAPTER 6 - EVERY MAN IS AN ISLAND

proved to me that the healing approach would be careful, taking into account my specific problems.

As I mentioned, the depression score didn't surprise me. I was in a depressive state and had had episodes. But the anxiety shocked me. I never thought of myself as anxious. Type A? Yes. Working hard to avoid obstacles? Yes. Turns out that *anxiety* is a different word for stressed out. That I could connect with. And with this shocking metric (top 4 percent—I mean, holy shit), it hit me: being type A was not my personality. It was not who I was. It was my defense mechanism. Action kept me stressed rather than aware of my anxiety and constant worry about what might happen. Ultimately, that unexpected and shocking score was one more invisible handcuff coming undone.

• • • •

Work schedules can be tiring, and there may be a ton of important things you want to get done. Wouldn't it be wonderful if you could just make sleep go away? You may even try to do that with some combination of willpower and energy drinks.

Well, forget it. You need sleep, and the older you get, the more sleep you need.

You need it to reenergize your body and allow it to heal. You may think you can push yourself to your limits, and when you're in your twenties, it may even appear possible. But once you're in your thirties, all those illusions fall away, and you need to get your rest if you want to be healthy. Good sleep will make a world of difference in terms of how much energy you have to get through the day; you may think you can squeeze out extra hours now, but you pay for those hours later when you get lethargic and collapse.

Once you reach your forties, you're going to need frequent blood work. You may be missing nutrients like calcium and magnesium, or your cholesterol may be too high, or there may be too much blood sugar. Are you taking vitamin D? Because most older adults I know do. (I live above forty degrees north. That matters. Check it out.) All of these will affect your mood, because your brain is part of your body. What happens elsewhere in the body affects your brain and thus

CHAPTER 6 - EVERY MAN IS AN ISLAND

your mood. You may also need supplements; check with your doctor about what could help, based on their assessment.

You might find this is a game of whack-a-mole. If you trashed your body to the extent that I did, you may chase internal pendulums as your body gyrates toward health. I got a bald spot out of nowhere the size of a golf ball. Biotin it is. I was working my way out of depression, and saffron was strongly recommended. You will go through times of turbulence. It's part of the process.

Blood work also functions as an early-warning system for problems in your body. Too often, people avoid blood work. But when they're hit with a health scare in their middle age, they hurry to see what's wrong and if it's something life-threatening, like cancer. Then, once they learn the problem, they change their lifestyle in a hurry.

It's better to find things out early so that if you do have something potentially life-threatening, you can act on it before you require drastic interventions like heart surgery or chemotherapy. Blood tests are also how you find out if you have diabetes or if you just need to change your diet.

Because your diet determines more than your waistline. Your mother was right: Don't eat too much sugar. Overconsumption of sugar leads to so many health problems; cutting back on sugar changed me for the better very fast.

Be warned, though: Cutting out sugar will be a major challenge, because the high-sugar processed food is so easy and convenient to get. You can take it out of the wrapper and chow down, and it tastes so good that you'll want more. The key is to throw out processed food along with the sugar itself. Once you come away from sugary processed crap, you won't want to eat it again because it will feel so gross. Think bricks in your stomach. Or falling back into a food coma midday. A good way to handle this is to prioritize protein, especially lean meats. Manage your protein intake and minimize your processed food.

On that note, track everything you eat. You cannot change your diet to be healthier without noting the specifics. Without tracking, if you cheat or slip and eat something sugary, it may compound as you get back into the habit. "One more wouldn't hurt," you'd tell yourself—and before you know it, you're scarfing down

Skittles and corn syrup again. Tracking what you eat helps you catch this before it becomes a problem and lets you get back under control. It'll also help you deal with any feelings of guilt about eating too much sugar when you can see exactly how much sugar you ate. By taking the guesswork out, you know what's going into your body as well as how much.

I can promise you that no diet remains unaltered if you accurately write down or use an app to track everything you eat. Once again, honesty and transparency are key.

But there's another way to help yourself, and it's one you may not have considered: the placebo effect.

The placebo effect is when something gives a physical or mental benefit merely because the user believes it could. It's why clinical trials for new drugs don't tell the test subjects whether they're getting the real treatment—they don't want the test subject's belief about the drug to influence the perception of the drug's effectiveness. Although you can't rely on the placebo effect to get you through a major medical problem, it can help with issues tied to your mental state.

A good example is acupuncture. It's based on using needles planted into your body to control the flow of your qi, or energy, to balance that energy out and thus heal your body. When you're experiencing it, it sounds more like a spiritual conversation than a medical one, to the point where people dismiss it as some kind of New Agey nonsense. From a scientific standpoint, it doesn't make sense, yet it works. When I had a ripped rotator cuff, acupuncture helped me deal with the pain.

I'm not saying acupuncture is fake. I'm telling you that you don't need to know how something works to receive its effect. And if in some cases it's your mind driving the impact, allow it.

Now let me show you the power of the placebo effect with an example from my own life.

To help manage my stress and anxiety, a physical therapist I trusted introduced me to a device called an Apollo. When I used it, I felt less stressed, and my sleep improved. The important thing here is that the only information I had about its effectiveness came from the company itself, so it was biased. But that didn't matter because I felt like it worked, so it did.

CHAPTER 6 - EVERY MAN IS AN ISLAND

Maybe it reset my parasympathetic nervous system, like their website claims. Maybe the buzz that goes off every so often makes me notice when I'm too stressed and so I take a moment to de-stress. Maybe it was sold well to me by someone I trusted, so my brain warmed up to it quicker. Whatever the reason, I slept better when using it. I didn't care why; I cared that it got the job done. When I put it on Energy Mode, my workout feels better, and that's all the evidence I need; I don't care about the details.

Sometimes all you have to do is trust your gut. You don't need stacks of scientific papers to tell you if something is effective or not—just go off how it makes you feel. If you feel better, it works. If you don't, it doesn't work. It's as simple as that.

If wearing black polos makes you feel more confident and close more deals, why would you wear anything else?

But buying some device isn't the only way to take advantage of the placebo effect. Here are some more great placebos that have helped me:

- *Walking in nature:* Simple walks outside did a lot for me, getting the blood pumping and improving my mood as I took in the fresh air.
- *Sound healing:* Just listening to pleasant sounds has put me at ease.
- *Incense, especially with candles:* Great smells improve the mood. Immediately.
- *Sunrises and sunsets:* Seeing the sun rise and set reminds me that time goes on, no matter what we're going through. And the universe paints in colors that are hard for anyone to match.
- *Seeing the Milky Way:* The size and beauty of the cosmos is enough to calm me down and fill me with awe. You have to go out of your way to get a good view of it too; you won't see it just glancing up from your house or in a large city due to all the light pollution. There's a primal connection and reaction that goes far beyond pretty stars.
- *Lyrics-free music:* Sometimes I just want to contemplate an emotion without the

CHAPTER 6 - EVERY MAN IS AN ISLAND

distraction of words. Also watch what some lyrics can do to your thought processes.

- *Binaural beats for meditation:* Being alone with my thoughts has done wonders in terms of clearing my mind. Might be placebo, might be for real. But meditation feels easier.
- *Chimes:* Chimes make a peaceful and gentle noise, and sometimes you need peaceful and gentle to get through a stressful day. Who's pissed off while chimes sound?
- *Taking in less news:* If it bleeds, it leads. The news is made to scare you so that you keep clicking and watching, afraid that whatever they're talking about will endanger you. It doesn't help that every so often, they're right. Honestly, fuck the news. Go do something closer to home, heart, muscle, or wallet.
- *Someone praying for me:* Whether or not you believe in God, this feels good and will push you forward during your day.

Each of these falls into a simple category: *If I do this, will I live better?* In my experience, they work every time.

That's all the evidence I need. I don't require multiple peer-reviewed studies, or expert opinion, or any other form of permission from someone with extra letters after their name. If I do it and I feel better, then it works, full stop. Its effect on me is all the evidence I need. My relationships improve. I can work smarter and harder. That's the power of the placebo. Don't underestimate it; your mind is more powerful than you may think. It's amazing what simple belief can do—and we're so quick to discount it because there's no study or other proof.

Here's another action else that benefits from something like the placebo effect—finding a good therapist.

Finding a good therapist is a lot like finding a good plumber or a good roofer—you'll discover them (best) through personal recommendations or existing relationships. But even so, you have to see if the therapist is a good fit. Do you feel confident dumping all your horrible secrets on this person? I've seen people go through three or

CHAPTER 6 - EVERY MAN IS AN ISLAND

four therapists and keep saying that they're not the right one.

In many ways, it's like a date.

How do you know you've found the right one? If you get more and more honest. A good therapist won't judge you or go overboard with advice; there are other factors, but those tend to be the biggest ones for most people. Female therapists focus more on your emotional history while male therapists focus more on action. One looks backward while the other looks forward. Depending on where you are in life, you may need each approach at different times (for example, I needed to look at my emotional wounds). I've had both. I've needed both.

Keep in mind that the point of therapy is not for the therapist to tell you what to do. Instead, it's for you to be honest about everything with a nonjudgmental party for the first time in your life. By verbalizing these things, you can move toward and through emotional closure. You've spoken it, so you've given life to it, and now you can heal it and let it be.

But speaking the truth is only the beginning; it takes multiple visits to reach the most painful wounds and unwrap those scars. Like an onion, there are all sorts of layers—hurt wrapped up in anger, anger wrapped up in defensiveness. It's relieving to speak what's on your mind and have someone listen to it who won't judge you. The reason your emotional wound was there in the first place was because it was too big to deal with when you first got it.

Getting to this point takes work. You must state the truth to your therapist when you talk to them. After you've done this, they should have a compassionate response, which shows that they care for your mental well-being. They need to be able to work with what you tell them.

As for how many sessions this should take, it's hard to know; however, a good rule of thumb for time is a year. If you're a man, being in therapy is probably not a thing you really want to do. It took me six months to peel back the onion layers and get to the bottom of what was bothering me. As you do this, you will find connections between things you never realized existed.

You also start with one parent and end with the other. For example, I started with my father (the obvious topic) and ended with my mother

CHAPTER 6 - EVERY MAN IS AN ISLAND

(less obvious but necessary) when I was seeing a therapist over my in-progress divorce. I had to both delve into my past and deal with the issues in the present day. Over these six months, I went every week; a few times, I went twice a week. Once I got to the end of that six months, I told the therapist that I didn't know what else to say, since I had revealed so much already. I wanted to know where to go from here. He told me that I did a good job because I came in ready to go. When we spoke of how to heal, we stayed on the positive path, as I wanted to know how to mend things with my boys and to heal my fractured relationship with my father.

This is why you need a year at minimum in therapy; you have to talk about your whole life up to that point and everything that got you into your current situation. Let's say you have a drinking problem. You're always keeping an alcoholic beverage handy, and you're cursing yourself because you're waking up hungover, you forgot your kids' events, or it's affecting your ability to provide for your family. You're not cleaning up this mess in a weekend. But you do have to clean it up, whether you want to or not.

Often, you'll hear the advice to man up, but this advice is not always given with your best interests in mind. However, bad people saying it does not make it any less true as a general rule.

In this case, manning up means digging into the deep well of your hurt. It's a hard thing for a lot of guys to do because we pride ourselves on our ability to handle tough situations without complaint. Too many men take a dip in the pool without committing, instead preferring to just improve their diet and find a hobby. They're partially healed, but it's not enough to stop there. To break from it, you have to stick with the therapy, like I did for a whole year. I didn't stop at the initial six months, because I knew that I needed more time to work it through.

The best part about this is that you don't have to do it alone. You need a community who will support you.

It doesn't have to be any kind of religious or spiritual community; I'm not nagging you to go to church. But communities are common ways for people to heal. For example, there's the well-known group called Alcoholics Anonymous but also groups like CrossFit for people who want

CHAPTER 6 - EVERY MAN IS AN ISLAND

to improve their physical condition, or nonprofessional sports teams, or any number of other social activities done in groups. If you're a man, you'll benefit most from all-male groups, but such groups are frowned upon in the modern day and thus will be harder to find. But if you can discover such a place and it isn't toxic to you, it will help you quite a bit.

In community, you will find peace in the eye of a paradox. Each of us lives wildly different lives in the details of our progression of steps through life. Yet you will hear your pain coming out of the mouths of others, of everyone. And not just pain but fear and anger. Critically, you will share your shame. As your heart breaks at times for your fellow human, you will find your heart breaking more and more for one critical person: you.

No one said making yourself OK would be easy, but it is necessary, and now you have the tools you need to take you down that hard road.

CHAPTER 7

MASCULINE SPIRITUALITY

To live is to suffer; to survive is to find some meaning in the suffering.

—Friedrich Nietzsche

Addicts aren't just wounded. And it's not just the father wound. It's a God wound. Like Nietzsche said, "God is dead." Without a transcendent value structure built into, on top of, underneath, or within our lives, there is no hope. Life is suffering. Punishment. Without hope of redemption. It's the worst. So addiction gets deeper. And if you had a problem, that problem becomes an obsession. Many nonaddicts quickly become addicts—or aspiring addicts. The only comfort is the chemical buzz of distraction. That works until it doesn't and won't anymore. Some people call that rock bottom. It's where you meet God. My hope is that you meet him (or her or they or it or whatever the hell works for you) on the way down. Either way, meet God, the Universe, Source, or maybe Higher Self.

In my own spiritual journey, I had a mentor who told me the main reason people study spirituality is to be happy. Isn't that interesting? So many of us look happy in public or on social media, or try our best to, but in truth we aren't happy and don't know how to actually be happy besides fake smiling for Instagram.

You meet all types of people in rehab and in therapy. You can tell when some healer or helper is living from a store of calm strength and, yes, even happiness. Theirs is an ongoing process, one they must maintain to keep their current level of satisfaction. That's why they're there.

On the way down or out, they found the answer to life, the universe, and everything—the answer for them personally at least.

I need to get direct and clear on something: Spirituality is different from therapy. Therapy should end; it's not a crutch to lean on for the rest of your life. Because once you've identified and validated the feeling that brought you to therapy in the first place, you must leave it behind (by bringing it home). By that point, you know what you have to do—and only you can do it. We may have had a deep need for validation, but there's no reason to dwell on it. It's OK now. Let go. Move on. Walk your path.

Spirituality is different; this is an ongoing process to work through all the continuous challenges life brings (because the challenges never stop coming, no matter how well you're doing). *The Creative Act* by Rick Rubin states that essential to spirituality is creativity; because you are imitating the acts of the creator, you are living a life of active prayer—and imitation is the sincerest form of flattery.[3]

---

3 - Rick Rubin, *The Creative Act: A Way of Being* (New York: Penguin Press, 2023).

But there are those who have trouble with the God thing. I get it. You might feel apathetic toward God because of injustice in the world or pain in your own life. You might call yourself an atheist, or you might be less *God doesn't exist* and more *God doesn't care*, a bit like an ex-spouse or a neglectful parent. That's fine. I'm not going to try to move you, if that's you. Rather, I want to give you a little push toward creativity for its own sake. You don't need a strict, divinely inspired code to tap into energy, meaning, and transcendence.

For the believers and for the devout, we need to reframe religion, tradition, and spirituality as not just a woman thing. Because that's what it is and has become for many in the Western world, and it feels effeminate for men. Because it is. Contemporary Christians, for example, do not live as heroic knights winning battles and living with honor. Many live the modern Protestant Jesus-is-my-boyfriend version of the faith. It's soft and inoffensive, the preacher is Tony Robbins lite, and there is palpable fear of confrontation. At the time of this writing, there was a viral video on social media depicting male worshippers at an evangelical megachurch dancing and prancing about like dainty ballerinas.

Modern spirituality worsens further when we move out of the Abrahamic faiths and get into the New Age. This spiritual-but-not-religious worldview tends to be perpetual therapy, with Eastern mysticism mixed in with ideas on "letting the oneness of the universe come inside you." OK then.

Meanwhile, you just sit in your feelings, letting them envelop you rather than resolving them and moving on like a man. All is one, brother, so it's OK to sleep around and eat mushrooms—no dogma about chastity and self-denial here, man.

This whole message repels men with a testosterone level above a bare minimum threshold. That's OK. In fact, that's good and correct. Because it's OK to be male. Being male does not make you pathological, toxic, or problematic.

However, religion and spirituality in their popular modern forms are presented under feminine light. In spite of gender-isn't-real messaging, men *do not* take to feminine approaches, and as a result they tend not to take religion or spirituality seriously. This isn't a matter of being some rippling muscle-bound caricature who shoots small animals in the front yard and drives a pickup truck through the back; it's about having a more active problem-solving approach to things rather than stewing in one's feelings all the time.

Remember how I mentioned dealing with your feelings by validating them and moving on? That's the typical masculine approach. You don't need endless validation, as feminine-facing forms of faith tend to offer. Masculine spirituality says, "Enough is enough," then moves on. Even if there is insufficient resolution. The feminine needs closure; the masculine does not. Masculine spirituality does not try to reconcile everything. Like being furious about something and not wanting to be furious. The resolution is allowing both, not trying to combine them or make sense of the conflict. The masculine is able to exist in this tension into perpetuity, for to be a man is to feel the tension, to live the tension, to *be* the tension. In response, the masculine says,

CHAPTER 7 - MASCULINE SPIRITUALITY

"It is what it is," and accepts without judgment. It is what it is.

I could get conspiratorial as to why manhood has been jettisoned from modern faith. I think it has more to do with perception. That is, spiritual practices or qualities such as kindness, compassion, intuition, and a nurturing spirit are all what? Feminine. Nothing wrong with that . . . *for women*.

At the same time, it's unwise to go too far in the other direction—the life of an agnostic ascetic. Modern life is already isolation, especially for men; we're all alone together (perhaps this is why messages about being one with the universe have such pull nowadays). When a man gets addicted to drugs or women or, hell, validation, it's like he's in solitary confinement, stuck in his own head with nothing but more of the same to numb the pain. To function and to win as men, we need community, and we need meaning; life is hard and then you die is not enough to push anyone forward.

The big questions get answered with *spirituality*, an overloaded word drained of impact.

These questions are pointing toward your personal salvation, and that salvation is for you and you alone to fully define. How can I be happy? Is there a God? Can I touch divinity? How? And a question that haunted me for years: What the hell really matters? What is *meaning*?

I thought for a long time that meaning had to be found. Like meaning was out there hiding from me. Kind of like looking for God as a gray-bearded old man on top of a mountain. And much like God (or at least the trail of divinity), I ultimately found meaning inside but only long after beating my head against the world, demanding it answer me.

For men, salvation is found through action. Contemplation is not enough. Looking outside oneself is part of the journey, but it is not the foundation or the destination. Meaning is created, lived, discovered. *You* are the meaning. Take the first step and start finding it.

You don't discover meaning like it's a street address. You discover meaning as if you are the road itself. Forever off to new adventures and pit

CHAPTER 7 - MASCULINE SPIRITUALITY

stops along the way. Discovering meaning is discovering yourself, literally.

But how can a man find this masculine spirituality? This question fits squarely in the feminine frame, ironically, as if there is still someone more qualified out there ready and willing to tell you what to do. There isn't. There's no one right way for everyone, but there is an approach that helps: Find an opportunity to take action with the right tools in an environment of challenge, not ease. Men function best in this condition. As many wise spiritual men have said, "If a church makes you feel totally comfortable, you're in the wrong church." And so whatever challenging faith looks like for you, the correct spiritual path is uncomfortable because it pushes you to fight your way through and prove your strength. It also has to be aligned with your goals so as to make you want to change; you'll find that whatever you're doing now is not what you wish to be doing. That is good. That is correct. That is masculine spirituality.

Next I'll share a few resources that have helped my experience. Some will work for you.

Others not so much. You'll notice emphasis on action, with the integration of contemplation, openness, and connection. But the key word is *action*. These are things we *do*, not just *feel*. It's OK to be a man. Do man shit. Sometimes that's thinking. But then it's acting. Doing. Moving. Making things happen. Do and feel. Here are ways you can do both.

An excellent, timeless tool is meditation. Don't think of it as just sitting cross-legged with your eyes closed; meditation includes a broad category of techniques to relax your mind, such as better ways to sleep, certain forms of self-talk, and even just being alone with your thoughts (for example, walking without earphones on). Life pulls our thoughts in various directions; being able to relax and make sense of them is a great way to help us heal our psychic wounds. Some of these meditation tools resemble yoga for the mind. Some are guided by others rather than done alone.

Meditation is ideal for driven type A people because we're comfortable living in our own mind. I'd go so far as to say that we get paid for

CHAPTER 7 - MASCULINE SPIRITUALITY

it, get applause for it, and even win in love. We value ourselves quite a bit, giving us a degree of mental protection. Meditation even allows us to take action in an emotionally safe way.

Let me explain. You create positive feedback loops and stop negative feedback loops by placing your mind in a healthy state. When you've spent a decade beating yourself up, drinking too much, and being ashamed, meditation is spiritually going for a walk (and it can include physically going for a walk too). You don't even need to have a spiritual or a God-believing outlook for this to work; think of it as a sort of hypnosis instead.

By the way, affirmations are a great tool to hypnotize yourself into a more productive way of thinking. If you tell yourself all the time that you do it, then you'll do it. Effective affirmations capture the negative thought, de-power it, then respond with a positive affirmation that eclipses that thought. Neutralizes it. Overshadows it. Replaces it. Because the reframe is better than the previous frame. For example, "I hate that I'm divorced; I never thought I would be divorced.

This sucks" can become "I am a free man again; I never thought I would have this chance. I get a do-over." Notice how more empowering and activating the latter feels as you read it. Read it again. Amazing. That's an affirmation; you *affirm* the superior perception of a given event. All reality is to us human beings is our perception. Choose your own perceptions; create your own reality.

Finding the right community also helps men like us experience masculine spirituality because, frankly, we need to get the fuck over ourselves.

Look, you're not the only one going through problems, and it doesn't help you to stay in your own head all the time. You'll be surprised by how many people have taken different paths, all to reach a similar place; more than once, I have heard my words coming out of someone else's mouth. Often, you're buried in a pit of shame, and that demoralizes you, making you doubt any action you take. But hearing that others are going through the same struggle and want to solve it breaks through that demoralization.

But within these communities, spiritual woo stuff is sometimes brought up, and the men often say no to testing any of the ideas or processes suggested due to how feminine that spirituality appears. Still, if you get over that hump, it can be helpful. Transformative. Community puts you in a humbler place around your problems. You judge yourself less. It builds your compassion, because when you can imagine yourself in the same circumstances as someone else, being compassionate becomes easy. When I went to rehab and spoke to other driven type A men, I could imagine myself in circumstances much like theirs. But even then, it was hard for me to let myself off the hook.

Talking to others also lets you see different ways you could approach your problem. There are a million ways to handle your problem, so most times you don't know where to go next. Just having someone list a bunch of suggestions gives you something; even better is hearing how other people handled the problem, because then you have a proven road map that you can adjust to your own circumstances.

Another tool that can help you is the reading of holy books. This isn't to convert you to that holy book's belief system but to give your mind something to wrestle with other than yourself. It keeps you from beating yourself up and focuses you on the text before you, espousing smaller or larger truths that may very well apply to your life. Considering that most of modern society ignores religion when it does not actively shun it, holy books may broaden your perspective. You'll find that going to the source, without any third-party interpretations or politicized commentary, cuts away all the baggage that our culture has built up.

Of course, traditionally sacred texts aren't the only kind of book that can have a profound effect. I read Cheryl Strayed's memoir, *Wild*,[4] then went on a one-month hike when my marriage was at a low point. It took me ten days to empty my mind. I had to chew on my hopes, my dreams, and my fears, especially for what could happen to my children should we divorce. On that journey, I realized that I hated living in Tahoe at that point in my life, even though everyone around me said

---

4 - Cheryl Strayed, *Wild: From Lost to Found on the Pacific Crest Trail* (New York: Vintage, 2013).

CHAPTER 7 - MASCULINE SPIRITUALITY

I was living the dream. I hated living full-time in a place that everyone said was gorgeous. But why was that? Because I could no longer be the type A person I had wanted to be. I had no reason to push hard.

Another book I read on that hike was *The Lost Symbol* by Dan Brown (of *The Da Vinci Code* fame).[5] Something I find interesting about his books is that he writes a list of three to four things that are true before diving into the fiction. For example, in this book, he proclaims that the Institute of Noetic Sciences is real. Indeed, the book's (fictional) heroine is a research professor there. Her character made some outlandish comments, and the book overall inspired me the way a holy book would. When I came back from the trail, I read the institute's actual research reports—and one was a decade-long study on how consciousness affects random number generators. One thing they did was set up an international network of random number generators, and they noticed how the randomness got less random during global upheaval like big

---

5 - Dan Brown, *The Lost Symbol* (New York: Anchor, 2009).

political events, with the theory that there's a time when human consciousness shares a similar perspective, a resonance. They noticed that the highest degree of nonrandomness was on 9/11. You can question the conclusion, or all of it. But this research made me question our assumptions around how consciousness works.

Two months after I read that research, I attended the Science and Nonduality Conference in San Jose, California. The point of the conference was to ask in what ways does science point to God (if at all) and how all of our questions tie into consciousness. As an example of the sorts of ideas discussed there, the English physicist Rupert Sheldrake pointed out the two-slit experiment done using quantum particles. In this experiment, if you don't measure the particles, they act as waves, but if you do measure them, they act as particles. However, he didn't stop there; he proposed that the fundamental basis of reality is consciousness—that is, consciousness comes even before the material world. Such a perspective challenges everything you thought

CHAPTER 7 - MASCULINE SPIRITUALITY

you knew about the world, though, to be fair, his theories lack broad acceptance.

The point isn't whether you believe any of these hypotheses; rather, it is to give men like us a framework for transcendental or even spiritual experiences. It forces us to go outside ourselves and to find out how much we don't know. Sacred books will do that. So-called secular reads will do that even more. You'll be surprised from which sources you'll encounter transcendence. Popular nonfiction and fiction alike may very well be that for you too. It doesn't have to say *Bible* to be close to holy for your spiritual journey.

But some people use chemical help to do that, to shatter the mirror of materiality. I explored psychedelics because, by that point in my life, I already believed that we were more spiritual than material. But I wanted to know more. A lot more. (Approach this with care and seek out professionals. None of this is a recommendation. Either you feel called to it or not. Tread with caution.)

I took DMT (dimethyltryptamine), and it ruptured my fear of death. It became clear to me in those fifteen minutes that we're conscious and that the body is just a temporary stop. I went flying over a fractal meadow and got to what felt like the end. Although my life wasn't reviewed, I saw my life visualized in front of me. It looked like a movie reel thrown in the air, just hovering in space, each frame picturing a moment in my life.

I thought then that I had died, and I was looking at the prophesized life review. I was less sad than I would have expected because the whole experience felt like it was behind me, and I wanted to go do a new life again. However, I didn't get to because I landed back in my body. That experience, however, was no ordinary physical body experience. All throughout, there was no feeling of a body, or taste, or touch. Yet it was more real than real.

A friend of mine worked with ibogaine (extracted from a West African herb), so I chose to try it too. I'd heard it had the most success for people struggling with heroin addictions. This friend of mine, in a spiritual circle I was in, healed his drug addiction through ibogaine. I took this herb the day after I did DMT, and what I saw were geometric patterns. Although it wasn't an experience like DMT, I left that place feeling rebooted and very calm. That said, I had an unusual experience compared to what others had.

I went there because I wanted to see if it could help me deal with my alcohol addiction. Doing DMT the day before may have messed me up, but I'm not sure; it's one of those weird things you look back on and you're unclear whether it helped or it didn't. The next substance I tried was microdosed psilocybin, because it's supposed to soften your ego, mixed with lion's mane to help your brain heal. But psilocybin wasn't the real kicker. That prize went to ayahuasca.

The thing with ayahuasca is that you have to show up clean. For years, I never managed to make it happen because I was on and off with alcohol and nicotine. I was strongly advised that I even had to get off caffeine to make this work. Once I mustered the courage to show up clean, I was warned that ayahuasca was a grueling, formidable experience. It is extremely challenging. Nonetheless, I went through with it.

(I need to stress that this option is *not* for everyone. I do not recommend it. It works for some and is awful for others. Approach with caution.)

The first phase of ayahuasca is a purging experience. The actual taking of the substance hits you hard and quickly from the start. Most people throw up; lucky for me, I did not. There's a massive amount of sweating; I had to wash my clothes before I left, because everything I wore smelled like sweat and detox. You purge out the back of you too, so it's even more gross than this.

After a lengthy phase of physical releasing, I went into an ego-death experience. For a long time, I knew I had to be an active listener and to broaden my boundaries to get at the truth. However, the ayahuasca gave this space a form I could sense. It made my ego melt away as I was embraced by a divine presence. It's hard to put into words the infinite love I felt, a love I couldn't even imagine. I was open to what the universe wanted from me. Afterward, I wrote "Infinity loving itself infinitely everywhere forever." That is what I experienced, times nine thousand.

CHAPTER 7 - MASCULINE SPIRITUALITY

I knew from therapy that I'd built up protective mechanisms around myself when I was young, so I took that opportunity to heal, hug, and forgive that little boy and open myself up to new possibilities. What happened is that any doubt I ever had about the existence of divinity went away. I don't know it all, but I know God is there. Is here. I kept in mind the Chinese farmer fable, the famous little story about the wise man who refuses to accept life as good or bad but as maybe. We don't know what's going to happen. What we can know is that life right here in this moment is a gift. And yet it is a neutral gift. Not bad or good. It just is, and it is what we make of it.

My journey brought me to neutral. It brought me to balance. I had to work hard to get there. You will too. The work is worth it. If it weren't hard, it wouldn't be worth it. And that is masculine spirituality.

CHAPTER 8

REACHING OK

The only journey is the one within.
—Rainer Maria Rilke

We don't know how to be human and not suffer. Throughout childhood and early adulthood, we absorb a stack of values and beliefs. We run off into the world ready to conquer. Many do. I did. Yet we find ourselves in middle age and life sucks. It feels 2D when it should be 3D. Nothing went how we hoped or planned. Maybe our kids hate us. We hate ourselves. We face divorce. Our careers suck the life out of our souls. *We are not OK*. I'd love to have had a life I prized. But to be honest, I just wanted to be *OK*.

Getting to OK is a decision, not a desire. One needs discipline (to do the work and make progress). And you need a lot of flexibility, a lack of "religion" when it comes to what you are willing to do, be, or do and be different.

Overall, I went from being willing to try new things to being willing to try just about anything if there was a good reason it might work. This story was the pinnacle. From total soul crushing to out of the valley of darkness. Lack of religion *and sticking with my decision* were my saving graces.

In total, I went to detox four times. My fifth time to get cleaned up was my first and only where I stayed in rehab for thirty days. This was a really big deal, because I had to finally face my sons (and my ex, for that matter), as I hid my detoxes from almost everyone.

When I got out, I felt fantastic. I was doing a long list of the things you do to be healthier, feel better, and have more energy. Meanwhile, there was a substantial list of things I was *not* doing

CHAPTER 8 - REACHING OK

that was equally important. For ten weeks, I felt like a new, younger, healthier man. I was on fire.

Then I felt the lights go out. It took thirty-six hours before the switch was fully flipped. I set into a depression that lasted months. I was crushed. This meant I was not OK (again). And drinking was on the horizon (pretty quickly but kept in check).

I went to my backup therapist because my main help was on vacation. This guy had watched me over the years, and I think he had a different perspective, given we would work together occasionally instead of routinely. He said some words that freaked me out, including *bipolar*. And when I dug into the symptoms, I could see why.

The point of the story is that this was crushing and terrifying. I was crushed because I felt betrayed postrehab. I was doing *everything* I was supposed to. I desperately did not want to end up drinking again, but I felt certain that was coming given the debilitating depression. And I was terrified that he might be right. That meant psychiatrists and their recommendation of drugs. That meant . . . what, exactly? I was fucked for life?

• • • •

Having gotten this far in this book, you know now how my story transpired. I was not, in fact, fucked for life. I have done the work of unfucking. I had a problem, and it was OK to admit it. It's OK to admit you have a problem so that you can deal with it.

I stayed with my decision and kept at it. That was my foundation. That was my salvation.

• • • •

There are a small few who walk fairly comfortably through life. I am finally becoming one of those people. Life isn't meant to be a prison; it truly is a gift. In my opinion, if you don't feel the gift of life, you have the problem this book set out to begin resolving. So the hope is that you are soon to be no longer one of those people. I'd guess 90 percent of everyone over thirty-five has this problem. Midlife crisis exists for a reason: It's life's way of saying that you fundamentally have it wrong. Healing is to at least get that bullshit out. We've done some flushing with this book so far, but we want to prevent backwash.

CHAPTER 8 - REACHING OK

There are only two feedback loops in life—negative and positive. This book was written to stop the negative one. Stop the backsliding, the digging deeper. What happens now as you stop the negative loop and begin the positive loop?

To do that requires *decision*. Reading and comprehending is not enough.

- *Decide* you will change. That you won't be religious about how. That life isn't meant to be only suffering.
- *Accept* that you don't know how to be human *and* to be OK.
- *Decide* that you will question all assumptions, *try* anything that works, and get *out* of your comfort zone.
- *Accept* that it won't be quick.

When you decide actively, you tell your subconscious who you are now (and thus who you will be) versus just kind of reading, hoping, waiting, seeing how things go. This is the difference between learning and living. It has been said that there is a difference between convincing someone of something versus converting them to believe and do it. This book has done a little convincing; my hope and intent is to convert you to a new way of living, but this is something only you can do. Everyone is always and only ever self-converted. That is how it is effective. I can believe this book works. You can, too, but only by doing it.

Agency is a muscle. Don't wait for perfection to change. Keep building it. Check the trend line in the rearview mirror. Compounding change adds up.

Small hiccups along the way? Analyze with brutal honesty. But self-flagellation is poison. You can handle the worst. Your worst. If it comes up again. Addicts think they are weak. And yet there is evidence everywhere that they are immensely strong. (Don't get outworked by a crackhead, as author and former professional boxer Ed Latimore says.) If addiction was or has been a struggle, then understand this: You will make it. You've got what it takes.

On this journey, I cannot tell you, recipe-like, what to do. No one can. This is the flaw of self-help because all help is self-help. It works only when you do it. You are both the wounded and the healer.

CHAPTER 8 - REACHING OK

But wait, Mark! You just told me chapters full of advice about what to do. What the F?

Yes, welcome to paradox. Welcome to being an adult and embracing life as it is instead of how you wish it would be. There are many questions with conflicting answers. You must seek out healers and aid and advice. And you must make every piece of it your own. Embrace what works for you and feel the healing begin inside of you. I can tell you that making a decision to change—truly deciding—is the beginning.

Healing happens circularly. I thought I was done with this. Truths deepen. Wounds have phases of healing and scarring. Life scratches at the wounds. Old triggers, defenses, and suffering return. Plus, you add a bit of chaotic randomness to the process. That is, there is no one way throughout. Your exact path has never been walked and will never be repeated.

But we can share the map.

We can walk this road together.

We can come home to our true selves and leave the mask behind.

We want the ego to heal. We don't want the ego to adopt the healing as the answer itself.

This will happen often. Temporary adoption is natural. But look out for the ego to seize therapy, CrossFit, Alcoholics Anonymous, or whatever as the answer. It probably won't be. So I am cautioning you: be ready to kill the Buddha.

Ever heard that one before? "On the road to enlightenment, when you encounter the Buddha, kill the Buddha." What? How? Find the healers and gurus. Listen to the many, many Buddhas. Find your own lessons, your own Buddha, make it yours. Whatever the *it* was that your Buddha taught. Do not allow your guides to become *the* way. *You are the way*. You are not Jesus; you are YOU. Living life is becoming the *Dao*. Being in the flow is then as simple as singing your song among the choir of life.

Understand how powerful you are: You are consciousness. You are the beginning and the end. You live in the middle of a hallucination. You seek that which you look for. Filtered through your value hierarchy. There is no direct knowledge. Only experience of it. Perception. In fact, the simulation theory is a great way to hold the truth, especially if God is a four-letter word. (For the atheist reader: Say there's no God, so how do you connect to reality? For me, I can rest in divine or creative consciousness. For you? How about the wise inner parent? The contemplative pool of creativeness? You'll figure it out. Find your way.)

What matters to you most defines how you approach, see, react, and interact with the world. (These are your Gods, whether you like 'em or not.) Bonus points? All of this is likely invisible to you in your subconscious. You've got to face this shit. Actions scream your truth. Thoughts are worth what you paid for them.

At your core is you. If you can't pick God, what will you pick? Start with the greatest good for you and those you love. (As Jordan Peterson says, "Clean your room."[6] Then take care of your family. Then your community. Let the rest of the world go for now. You've got a mess to clean up.)

Take all this slowly, because it is slow. Patience is a virtue and gives the universe time and space to work with you. You simply can't nail everything down. Take the big bang, string theory, dark matter, and dark energy. A hell of a

---

6 - Jordan Peterson, *12 Rules for Life: An Antidote to Chaos* (Toronto: Random House Canada, 2018).

lot of words to say, "I don't know." There will be many more of those along the way. The ego wants to know, it has to know, but it doesn't need to. Consider having all the answers and feeling miserable, contrasted with not having the answers and being OK with that. It doesn't mean being selfless or building up your ego again. It means sitting with the question. It means having cognitive dissonance and being OK with that—and that alone helps the dust settle and clarity arrive. "I don't yet have all that I want in life, and yet all that I have, I want." That is your attitude, your outlook, your inner peace.

Men can have inner peace too. It is the default state of man; in fact, it took a lot to move us away from peace—and it takes monumental effort to get us back there. Reading one book is not enough, but it is the beginning of something. It shows that you take this seriously enough to set your vector in the right direction for who you want to be, what you want to do, and how you want to feel. Recall the "Be water" quote by Bruce Lee. What does water do? It goes where it must. It does not resist. It is what it is. It changes state when the environment demands it. It doesn't wash uphill. It doesn't freeze in the hot desert sun, as much as it might "want" to do either. It is water. It is present. Be water.

To be water is wisdom. Wisdom is acting from the present moment unencumbered by the bondage of the past or by anxiety over what may come. Wisdom is also called the divine. Or light. Or the divine light. Pick your metaphor; pick your woo. It doesn't need to be true in a literal sense; it just has to work.

For me, prayer does. And so I will close with this prayer:

I pray for you to find God, even if you wish I would not. This book is one big prayer for the Light inside you and the Light in the world. At the core of your heart is your soul. And the fabric of your soul is Love. Love is divine. The foundation of all divinity is the Love that is God beyond word or explanation. What could be a greater belief or value? (Jordan Peterson quote: "I do my best to act as if God exists.") Drop the finger-waving God. Bring in your wise inner Father. Let that Light be your Guide. Even if you are faking it.

You have to do this for yourself. Not for your spouse. Not just for your kids. That is a version of wanting versus deciding. Shoulds versus the clarity of *I will do this no matter what*.

You thought you read this book to feel better. You read it to learn the truth.

What that truth *is* and *was*?

That's up to you.

Your truth doesn't have to be true; it just has to work.

EPILOGUE

BETTER THAN OK (AND THE PATH TO GET THERE)

Decisions, not conditions, determine what a man is.
—Viktor Frankl

We want the act of *deciding* to be smooth. Make a decision? Be done. I WILL NOT DRINK AGAIN! And voilà! We want the clarity of knowing we are done. We want control over our addictions and ourselves. Mostly, we want the benefits ASAP—and to then be free of suffering and the embarrassment of failure.

Yet deciding can only be made reality through agency and action. At first, as a former slave to our addiction, we find our agency weak at best. Real success comes from strengthening one's resolve through repeated positive action, especially in the face of temptation.

Yet failure, much like shit, happens. We take these failures hard. We see the missteps as indicative of a character flaw. Impostor syndrome kicks in. Maybe we never really changed. Maybe we are as damned as we always assumed.

Or . . .

This is now your chance, the rubber meeting the road, so to speak. You may not like it; hell, you definitely won't like it. You'll want to rip the head off well-intentioned people who foolishly tell you the truth: this is an opportunity.

Who do you want to be? What will determine who you truly are? How you respond to failures will answer these questions.

I left rehab at the end of a bright, warm July with a skip in my step. Maximizing positive feedback loops. Minimizing all negatives. Exercising, wakesurfing, eating healthy, prioritizing sleep, drinking no alcohol. My usual therapy plus extra somatic therapy. I still had a few negative loops (i.e., nicotine, negative thoughts), but I was working on both. Working through urges, quieter now, almost daily but softened.

I made new friends. Started dance lessons to get out and be social without drinking (salsa and bachata; I prefer the latter). Made a new business friend to work on some deals with. Started working on a new restaurant (Perse, forthcoming near Beverly Hills, California). Began dating. Focused on being with my boys, one heading off to college soon, the other back to high school. Worked on my guilt for having had to leave in the first place.

I felt strong. The occasional urge wasn't that tempting. It helped being fresh out. It helped more just being on. I thought I was experiencing what addicts hope for: real joy. To some extent, that was true.

My birthday came along. Maybe that was the trigger. That birthday was my fifty-third. I found myself fairly reflective on my life. What was in the rearview mirror felt more like a technicolor disaster than success. Dating had been enjoyable but ultimately not fruitful. And my oldest had recently left for college.

I'll never know what or if there was a trigger. What I recall is this feeling that being on had turned off, like a switch. Something in me felt like gravity had increased, energy diminished, light turned dull. I knew something had changed, and it was wrong.

I hated having no motivation. I lost my oomph, and my work suffered. I was back to slogging day by day. The urges ramped. And I did succumb to them. I felt the failure and defeat completely.

My ongoing healer was on vacation (I don't use the word therapist for her. This work has moved well past plain therapy). Thankfully, I had someone else to turn to. He had been one of my teachers, both formal and informal. And he had seen me over the years, mostly during times of crisis, of which there had been plenty. I share this because I think this gave him a different perspective of me, more of the forest for the trees. Because when we met, he had quite a bit to share.

He was careful and compassionate. And firm. "Mark, have you considered that you might be bipolar?"

Horror and terror. Nausea and sweat.

But also a little hope. A quiet voice wondered if this would explain how difficult things had been. To put this in context, I had been more off alcohol than on it for the previous six years. I had done extensive therapy. A four-year spiritual healer program. Ibogaine. Satsangs. A random drum circle. Mistress Colette, for God's sake!

Yet I was crushed. Defeated. And 100 percent terrified of what the next conversation entailed. Who ya gonna call? A psychiatrist.

I am convinced my friend who shot himself in the skull did so because he was on mood medications for too long. I'll never know for sure. But my mind and body screamed with fear. I wanted help. I needed help. And I had no idea how to trust anyone with such a degree.

But I decided I was done with alcohol. Even in the midst of drinking again (but limited), I would not accept defeat. I would lean into this curve ball.

I spent weeks researching options. Thankfully, a friend suggested the Amen Clinic. After reviewing the website for maybe five minutes, I picked up the phone and asked a million questions.

They do prescribe, but they don't push drugs.

They do extensive testing first, including a 3D brain scan.

And they do extensive blood tests.

Not cheap. But I appreciated the patience of the staff. And the rigor of their approach. I told myself I would try everything but drugs, at first. I told myself this was worth the risk.

Cognitive tests.

Emotional tests.

Blood tests.

The brain scan was the most instructive. I had clear signs of surface trauma. The smooth surface was disturbed, like mashed potatoes. Then I was told I had a golf ball-size hole in my head with almost no blood flow. And finally, an overactive dopamine system (the thalamus).

Happily, my cerebral cortex looked surprisingly good. Then the psychiatrist said the magic words.

EPILOGUE - BETTER THAN OK (AND THE PATH TO GET THERE)

"I think we can help you."

He described my situation as a less severe case of professional football syndrome—that is, brain damage from repeated minor (or major) head trauma. My best guess is this came from skydiving. I have completed approximately thirty-seven hundred skydives. Some of those included rapid openings under canopy. Some were terribly quick, decelerating my body and my brain from 120 mph to nearly zero.

Think of it this way: 90 percent of the time when your chute opens, you get a relatively easy opening without trouble. I'll skip nonopenings. The rest are pretty fast. So 120 mph to almost zero is no joke. Some of those are sharp, like driving your bike into something immovable. A few of those are nasty. Thankfully, a very small percentage were like that. But 0.1 percent of 3,700 is four.

And one, the worst, was about ten years ago. I probably should have gone to the hospital. I broke into a full body sweat afterward. I could feel I was off, not thinking right. I had pulled a little high to the ground, in the saddle, over two thousand feet. I slowly steered around.

Something was off in my mind-body connection. What normally would feel joyful and free instead felt disconnected and flat. I landed far away from the others and made my confused way to the hangar. I knew I was done, and so did everyone else. That's the one I believe triggered me into my worst phase.

Next, my doctor explained that although the tests and commentary may all sound scary, Amen had a history of helping such head trauma-related injuries heal. The main magic? Hyperbaric oxygen therapy, or HBOT. He warned me it would take at least thirty hours of treatment to see a difference. At sixty hours, it was becoming obvious that healing was happening. Mood swings stopped. Past ninety hours, my daily craving at dinnertime disappeared.

If you've never struggled, this might be hard to impress upon you. The lack of craving changed my life. Now I have no problem not drinking.

I imagine this would be like tinnitus going away. Life went from maddening, requiring strength of will (which ultimately runs out), to simply maintaining a firmly held decision. I am, as they say, a new man.

EPILOGUE - BETTER THAN OK (AND THE PATH TO GET THERE)

I did come awfully close to giving up. I was demoralized by taking another drink. Terrified by the possibility of being bipolar. Furious that what had felt like a decision was called into question—a question of who I was at my core! The difference? Sticking through it anyway. Give yourself *time* to keep winning. Give yourself *grace*. Do both, and you just might find yourself better than OK.

I have.

You can too

ACKNOWLEDGMENTS

Lake Tahoe is astoundingly beautiful in the summer. My passion is to get out on the lake early to wakesurf before the parade of boats and tourists. Freshly baptized in the lake, I am grateful to be alive. I hold peace in my bones and gratitude in my heart. I welcome today, whatever may come. But not that long ago, I was on an accelerating slide toward death. I was suffering. I felt ashamed and terrified. I lost vibrancy. I never felt suicidal, but I understood why it's so terribly common.

Now? I am wildly thrilled that my parents chose to marry and have my two sisters and me. I am grateful to be alive. I am grateful for everything. I hold true praise for God.

If you read much of this book—hell, any of this book—you might find that surprising. But the journey does come full circle. It is with that hope and promise that this book was written. It would not have been written without the wisdom and love of those who went before me. I would like to acknowledge them now.

• • • •

Mom in heaven, thank you for this life, your love, and your guidance. You left us all far too soon. You suffered greatly. I am certain I was the cause of quite a bit of pain. And now as a parent, I get it, to the marrow of my bones: Being a parent is hard. You lacked support. You believed in me, and you loved me. You did your best. We are connected forever. I love you.

Dad in Southern California, thank you for this life. Thank you for the lessons you shared and the guidance you gave. Our path together was horrible. As you put it, we were at war. No more. I am proud of the work you have done these past decades. I know you love and care. And I understand what it means to live with horrific wounds and double-edged defenses. I had

ACKNOWLEDGMENTS

to find forgiveness for myself first. And then I could forgive you. We are connected forever. I love you.

To my immediate family and closest friends, thank you for sticking around and dealing with me at my lowest points. I know that was challenging, to say the least. I expect some to retain fresh scars. Much love and respect to each and every one of you. I owe you. Thank you, Michelle and Andrew, Alissa and David, Rose and Chris, Sanjay and Charlene, Jared and Siig, Michael and Kim, Reuel.

Many healers, teachers, counselors, and wise ones have helped and guided along the way. More than any, I want to thank the community A Society of Souls. Jason, thank you for founding the school and for the numerous books and works you have created. I still don't really grok how the hell you brought all of that together. We students are all grateful for you. I love your work, and I love you.

Eileen and Jeff, thank you both for being our teachers. The commitment you have to the work is astounding. More times than I can count, I recall the love and compassion you have for all of us. You're both just . . . so damn good at what you do! And thank you for asking me to help the newest class; it has been an honor. Love you both. Eileen, thank you for the years of healing work together. You are far more than any label I could apply; you are a healer through and through. My heart sings with gratitude and respect for you. And, Jeff, thank you for your healing help and support. Your advice wasn't always easy, yet it was always valuable and needed. You have my full respect as a man and as a healer.

Along the way, there were many others. For those I failed to acknowledge, I apologize. Thank you, Colette (see chapter 1), Bettina, Barbara and Mason, Roxana, Jonathan, Mary, Damon, Teddy, all my classmates at ASOS. And Arlene, Verlyn, Kerrigan, Charles and Tatiana, Micah and Michael, Cheryl and Emily.

Kat, thank you for your love and support. For quite some time, no one knew but you. And you gave me space for the roller-coaster ride that this effort became. Thank you for your patience and courage. I love you, my tip of the spear. See you at the chapel.

ACKNOWLEDGMENTS

How did the book happen? I don't know if I will succeed, but I wrote this book because I needed to give back. I am not trained in therapy. No Ph.Ds. I am not a guru. The book happened because I find redemption to be one of humanity's greatest strengths. I have been fortunate in many ways. I pray this book helps those in need.

This book could not have reached you without the support and guidance of Alison Beckwith. Thank you for your tireless effort to bring this book to its readers.

This book, in this form, with this power, simply could not have happened without Joshua Lisec. Far more than an editor, Joshua was my writing partner. I'll be honest: I am not the best writer, and I certainly am not fast. Joshua was critical in structuring the book and putting wood behind the arrow of what I worked to say. Check Joshua out, as you will hear far more from him. (As of this writing, he has just coauthored two New York Times bestsellers in back-to-back weeks.)

Finally, all of my love to Kai and Jude. This book would never have happened without you; I would not have found the strength to keep going.

But because I could not keep hurting you, and I would not abandon you, I put one foot in front of the other, even when I couldn't see what was in front of me. I love you both with all my heart.

Thank you all.

Mark/Dad
August 27, 2024

ABOUT THE AUTHOR

Mark Gogolewski is a serial entrepreneur, start-up adviser, investor, filmmaker, and father. Mark's notable exits and projects have included the successful sale of Denali Software to Cadence Design Systems for $315 million, the successful sale of Nvelo to Samsung for an undisclosed amount, the Tap Haus restaurant in Tahoe City, and the documentary *Buried*, which became the sixth most watched title on Netflix US during its first week of release. An avid skydiver with more than 3,700 skydives completed, Mark shared the world record in skydiving with

245 other flyers for the largest planned formation. Mark writes and speaks to groups of men and leaders on the inner world of the high performer. Follow Mark at www.markgogolewski.com.

www.ingramcontent.com/pod-product-compliance
Lightning Source LLC
Chambersburg PA
CBHW030454100526
44580CB00010B/124/J